Buccaneer and Advantura

To France in a Motorhome

Jon N. Davies

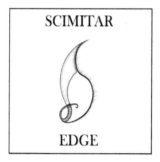

SCIMITAR

EDGE

Published by Scimitar Edge

An imprint of Purple Unicorn Media

ISBN 978-1-915692-12-2

For Mum and Dad

Who took us on Adventures

THANK YOU

To all the kind people in the fantastic community on Twitter/X who helped me over the past many months with identifying misspelled or illegible place names, and especially the location of unlabelled, or incorrectly labelled photographs.

This book is all the richer for you all.

Table of Contents

Introduction

In August 1978, we hired our first motorhome and went to Northumberland. A year later, in June 1979 we hired our second motorhome and went to Cornwall. In early 1980, we purchased what would become known colloquially as "the white van", a Bedford Buccaneer motorhome with a lift-up roof.

Early holidays continued to be around the United Kingdom, including an epic trip to Scotland in the Summer of 1981. In April 1983 we went one better, and crossed the Channel to drive from Normandy to Paris, and back. This holiday was recorded by way of alternating reports as homework my Mum and Dad set me and my sister.

A year later, with my secondary school I was back in Paris, and whilst this coach and hotel holiday does not ideally fit into this narrative, it was important in my personal experience of France.

In late 1985 we bought a second motorhome, a Bedford Advantura, a high-roofed one for me and my sister's growing bodies, and in the long Summer of 1986 we journeyed to France and Andorra. In this holiday, Dad had his dictaphone and would create an article from his spoken notes upon our return. My diaries of this holiday form a second record of events.

In the Summer of 1987 we again went to France, this time down the Western, Biscay coast. Dad's logbooks and my partial diaries form this record.

We were four – Dad, who worked for Thomas Cook, Mum, who was a teacher, myself born in 1970 and my sister, Beth, born 1972. At home, our 5th was Tandy, our cat, but we never took her on holiday!

The Buccaneer

Our first trip out in the Bedford Buccaneer was on the 5th February 1980 - I know that because I wrote a diary of the first few outings and holidays in it, presumably some sort of homework for me from my parents as it is ticked and corrected.

With the registration SNY 702 S, the motorhome had been first registered in March 1978, so was a little less than 2 years old when we bought it.

The Buccaneer with the roof up, my sister and I approaching

The seating was usually on either side of a central aisle, though it could be turned into a U shape, if more people were to be accommodated, such as my cousins on my Dad's side. A table could be erected in between the side benches for meals, though occasionally it was left up when travelling.

The cab included a cassette player and for long journeys Mum and Dad had bought a series of story tapes, what we would now think of as "audio books", aimed at all the family, including myths etc.

I was prone to travel sickness, so a seat that helped to ameliorate this was important. This was immediately behind the front passenger seat, with a view out of the central windscreen. My sister would sit opposite, behind the driver.

My sister slept above the cab, whilst I slept in one of the side-slung hammocks, Mum and Dad slept below when the seating and table area was made into a double-bed.

A rare interior shot, showing Mum in the middle, my aunt & cousin

If entered from the rear doors, the fridge and cooker were on the left hand side, and I especially remember the burnt sausages from our first attempt at cooking in the van – I even wrote in the 1980 diary book that I preferred them to normal sausages!

The right hand side held a small, rarely-used toilet, and the sink along from it, with the lift-up top.

The Buccaneer with the roof up, with Mum, and my tent

The Buccaneer parked up on the side lawn at 2 Juniper pending sale, 1986

Paris 1983

This diary was written by myself (aged 12 and a half) and my sister, Beth (aged 10) in April of 1983, taking it in turn, more-or-less, to write up the events of the day as they occurred. Each day is titled with the author of the diary entry.

I have attempted to match the photographs that exist to the diary entries, but a few have not been possible to identify. This one below of Dad "somewhere in France" being one of them!

We had got everything except the clothes in the previous day and, when the clothes were packed, Dad after looking up got in, fastened his seatbelt and turned the key. It made a spluttering noise but nothing happened. Dad muttered a load of nonsense, undid his seatbelt, threw his hat into the back, climbed out and asked for his hat.

The car was driven out of the garage and jump connected to the van. At about 10:25, we got going and had an uneventful journey until we broke down outside an underground station. Dad called the RAC and phoned Grandma to tell her about the breakdown.

We had three biscuits and a long wait before the RAC vehicle arrived. He had ginger hair and was smoking a cigarette. He poked around the bonnet and asked Dad to start the engine. When Dad did, the bonnet fell on his head. So, I had to get out and hold up the bonnet.

He got us started and we carried on. A few minutes before our second breakdown, Mum said, "It's smoother than ever."

At 1:45 we broke down inside the Blackwall tunnel. Dad phoned the police on an S.O.S phone and they arrived, towed us out and phoned the RAC. This RAC man took a long time to arrive but was a much more pleasant man than the previous one, and he fixed us and said that the trouble was a broken condenser.

We arrived at Grandma's at 4:30 P.M and soon had dinner/tea. I read until we left for Uncle Colin's at 7:30 P.M. We met everybody then at 8:30 P.M went back to Grandma's and read till it was bedtime. I had an uneasy night.

In the morning we (children) were woken by a telephone in my room. This was a signal from Mum and Dad for us to get up. We had big breakfast in which we were joined by Mum and Dad.

We (all 4 of us plus Grandma, Uncle Colin and his children) went to the second communion service. I did not hear all that much because of my cough. In church we had to go up and get blessed but the adults had some wine and pieces of bread aswell, because it was Easter Sunday.

After church the 4 of us and Grandma went back to Grandma's place and gathered up our things and put them into a plastic bag.

We went to Uncle Colin's (and Auntie Mickie's) for dinner and I had extra helpings of jelly but Beth chose to NOT LIKE it when she was told it had no sugar inside.

After dinner I read my book by Hammond Innes called Wreckers Must Die. I drew a plan of a U-boat base from it and also wrote the account for yesterday.

After that I started a new book called Most Secret. Beth was up in the greenhouse digging up the soil at Auntie Mickie's.

At 7-something we started to watch a film called Escape to Athena starring Telly Savalas, Roger Moore, Anthony Valentine and Stephanie Powers. This was about Nazi-dominated Greece in 1944.

While we were watching this, we had a buffet tea and most of the time leading up to tea Beth was bathing Uncle Colin's children.

After this, we went home to Grandma's in the middle of Pepys and went to bed.

In the morning, I woke up and finished my book which was I was half way through. I heard Grandma moving so I looked up. Grandma had just gone to the bathroom, so I started another book.

When we had both been to the loo, the doorbell rang. Grandma was getting washed and Jonny and I were still in bed. I didn't realise that it was the doorbell, so I jumped out of my skin. I suddenly realised that it was the doorbell, so, I answered it. Mummy and Daddy came in and we all had breakfast. I lazed around most morning not knowing what to do. Daddy was looking up Mr. Howard in the telephone directory, but they were out. I went into my bedroom and read, and then in came Daddy asked me if I wanted to go to Sainsbury's Home Care store. We went and it took us quite a while to find it. When we did eventually found it we tried to park. It was really crowded and all the cars looked as if they were going to knock everybody over. We eventually parked and went in. After we had a long look around, we went, we were looking for a shop for us to buy the food.

We couldn't find one so we went back to Grandma's house. We had dinner and then went up to Auntie Mickie's and Uncle Colin's house and played with the boys. When it was time for them to have their bath, I bathed them and washed their hair.

We were woken up by the alarm clock at half past 5. Grandma went to the bathroom while I decided to undo my plaits and brushed my hair. Then Grandma came out and I went in. After I was washed and dressed, Jonny went into the bathroom and Grandma and I started breakfast. When we had just had our cereal, Jonny came in. We all finished our breakfast and Jonny and I, packed our bags and brought our things into the lounge.

The doorbell rang and in came Daddy and Mummy. They had their breakfast and then went. It was about 7 O'clock by then. We went to Uncle Colin and Auntie Mickie's then to get the van.

We said goodbye to everyone and then we drove off. We went to Newhaven and we had to go through Brighton to get there and we went past the pavilion and the aquarium. When we got to Newhaven, we went to the port and we weren't sure whether we were a car or a lorry. We decided to be a car and a man said that it was all right. We queued up for ages and when we eventually got moving, we couldn't move. We couldn't move because the car in front of the car in front of us hadn't got anybody in, they seemed to have gone for a walk.

Daddy went to look for them and he brought them back so that we could move. When eventually we had got the car into the ferry and we were about to set sail, I looked overboard into the sea and the journey began. We sailed for roughly four hours. When we got to France, we drove out of the ferry and drove to a campsite. When we got there, we wanted the loo but when we saw them, we didn't fancy the French one and there was only one English one there.

In the morning we got up and got washed and dressed. Then we had breakfast and I had cornflakes. Beth had Coco Pops.

After breakfast we cleaned our teeth and set out for Rouen. We had trouble parking but managed it eventually.

We went through a door into the cathedral. There were little alcoves dedicated to different saints in which you paid 4 Francs (about 40p) to light a candle and to say a prayer.

There was a centre communion altar in which three sides were public and one was for the choir.

In a few of the alcoves there were confession boxes which, I guess, you went into it to confess.

After this visit, we went to find a coffee (café) shop but lost Dad when he paid a meter 1 Franc to stay half an hour longer. So instead of having coffee, we wandered round the old streets.

We got moving and had dinner outside a school where the board behind Mum's chair was broken mysteriously by Beth. We moved on out of Boniers and drove through countryside until we arrived at a camp site, just out of Paris and by the River Seine in Maisons-Laffitte.

We aimed for here because we needed a shop. At the shop, Mum bought some comparatively cheap red wine. Later on, we went to bed.

We awoke at 8:45 (but later discovered that we were an hour behind and when we thought that it was quarter to nine, it was a quarter to 10).

Maisons Lafitte Campsite, showing the railway and bridges over the Seine.

After the morning preparations, we walked up to Maisons-Laffitte station, bought 8 tickets (allowing for the journey back) and got a nice electric train and travelled to St. Lazare station (in Paris). We disembarked and walked outside. Outside we saw a coach from Congleton (near Biddulph) and Mum and Dad had a long chat to it. Dad also cine-filmed it and us. (*)

After the end of the talk, we walked to La Madeleine and walked round. In here also you could buy a candle and in a little room a lady was saying her confession. Above the altar were painting and sculptures. Dad also ventured down into the crypt.

After the church, we walked down to the Place de la Concorde and onto the Louvre. In the Louvre we eventually found (after a long tiring plod) the Mona Lisa by the famous Italian artist Leonardo da Vinci.

We walked out of the Louvre and found a café in which everybody else had pizza and I had a massive hotdog with two sausages and cheese. After paying the bill (billet in French) we went to an ex-Thomas Cook office and Mum and Dad had a talk to a man in (in English) who was sad to leave Thomas Cook. Anyway, he directed us to another office where we booked a trip around Paris for tomorrow with a 50% discount.

After this, we walked to the station, caught a train and arrived at our camp site. Then we went to bed.

*Correction by Mum:- This was actually later, outside the Louvre, in the Place de la Concorde

Place de la Concorde with the Eiffel Tower in the background

Place de la Concorde, showing the obelisk and fountain at the upper left

8th April 1983   Beth

We woke up, got washed and all that, had breakfast and cleaned up. We got the roof down, paid and left.

We drove down to the next campsite and we had to drive through the New Town. It was a peculiar place, with flats looking as if they were made of cheese, only they were blue. When we got to the campsite, they gave us a piece of wood with a number on. We parked, and went to catch the minibus and then bought the tickets. (You see, the minibus left the campsite at every 20 minutes).

When the minibus journey ended, we caught the metro to the Concorde station. When we got there, we walked to the Cityrama shop. At 2:30, we set off. We went to the Invalides and saw Napoleon's tomb. Then we went to the river Seine for a ride on a boat. While we were on the coach, driving to the different places, we went past lots of places and a man with a microphone was telling us about them. We passed under a lot of bridges in the boat then we went around a loop and came back to the jetty. We drove in the coach to the foot of the Eiffel Tower, then went up to the first floor. We came down again and went back to the coach. We waited 25 minutes for the Spaniards to come back but they didn't so we left them. We drove back to the Cityrama shops and caught the metro to the minibus stop. We caught the minibus back to the campsite, had tea, made the beds and went to bed.

First floor of the Eiffel Tower

View from the 1st floor of the Eiffel Tower looking down over the bridges of the Seine

We awoke and got dressed and ate our petite dejeuner. Then we got ready, paid and left the Bois de Boulogne campsite and drove out of Paris, through the countryside to Versailles. We parked in the rain and me, Dad and Beth walked up to the gate and went through it. We then walked up to a statue of a French ruler on a horse made out of bronze but was melting.

We walked through a passageway and into the gardens. There was a lake here which Dad said was where the king's fish came from. I took a photo of Dad and Beth in front of the "King's View".

Then we made our way back to the van and drove on. We came to an 'Auto Route' and had to pay to be allowed on it.

We went ¾ of the way and then went into a café service station thing and went to the toilet. Then we drove onto Chartres and parked near some coaches. We walked up to the cathedral in the rain. We entered the cathedral. My how dark it was! We walked round the cathedral trying to notice all the statues and things. We walked up some steps and entered a room. In this room, there were carvings falling apart and clothes and treasures.

After we had descended the stairs, we carried on round the cathedral and found a warm air thing which we rested on.

We walked out, visited a little souvenir shop, lost Dad and found him again. After this little bit of excitement, we visited PRINTEMPS where Mum bought some tissues. Then we marched on to a shop where we acquired eight sausages and two Quiche and then into another shop where we bought an extra tiny French loaf. We visited a little toy shop where I bought something. Then we started off and came to a campsite eventually and camped next to the toilets.

The photograph at Versailles, mentioned in the text, with Beth and Dad in the rain

At the Palace of Versailles, showing the front of the motorhome

We woke up next to the toilet block in a campsite called 'Cheval Blanc'. We did all the usual things and then set off for a nice ride in the sun to Fontainebleu Palace in Fontainebleu.

We couldn't go in the palace itself because it was closed and anyway, it was a museum. We couldn't go round the Diana Gardens or the English Gardens because they were closed as well. We went round the courtyards and went to the wall to look at the ducks that were in the dried up lake. We walked out again and went back to the van. We drove to a layby in the forest and had a meal. We drove on back to Paris and drove past the Notre Dame.

We stopped quite near the Arc de Triumph. We didn't go up it because there was quite a long queue, so we went back to the van where we had left Mummy. We then drove up to the Sacre Coeur but we didn't get out of the van, or even stop it. We did have a brief stop at the Sacre Coeur before the police waved us on. It was a big traffic jam going down the hill and on the pavement there was a family with a big dog (it was a Samoyed). Then we heard a police car in a hurry. It nearly ran over the lovely Samoyed. We drove then to a campsite in Beauvais.

The Palace at Fontainebleu

The Arc de Triumph from the motorhome

The Tomb of the Unknown Soldier, within the Arc de Triumph, Paris

Place des Ternes, Paris

We woke up, got dressed, ate our breakfast, washed up and Beth and I had a little play. After our play, we parked up and drove to the reception where Mum jumped out and paid. When she had clambered in, we drove to Beauvais and parked just outside the cathedral.

We then entered the cathedral. Inside we found a new organ had been erected because the old one had been destroyed in the Second World War by a bombing raid. We found a musical clock whose workings date back to 1302 and sat down to see what it did. Unfortunately, we looked at the wrong part. Also, inside was an exhibition of photographs which were about the cathedral. Two showed the cathedral surrounded by ruins during the Second World War.

After we had finished looking, we went out of another door and found ourselves opposite a toilet. Mum paid 1 Franc and we all went to it. It had a funny place to wash your hands and had a warm air blower. It knew when it was in use by a balanced platform. It also cleaned itself.

After this, we walked back to the van and drove to Compiegne where we went to an information office and changed some money. We visited a shop or two and Beth and I bought an ice-cream. The information office was in an old building with a very old clock which every time it struck 3 figures moved around. This had the oldest striking bell inside it.

We drove on to Reims, viewed the cathedral through the window, and then went on a long search to find the campsite.

It was called Airhotel so we looked at the airport but eventually found it in an industrial area.

That night I had a nightmare about a motorway or something horrible.

Beauvais Cathedral

Reims Cathedral

Ambleny French National Cemetery, between Compiegne and Soissons, and thus on the road that leads eventually to Reims.

We woke up, and did all the usual things, before we set off. We drove to Reims Cathedral, but we couldn't look around it because there was a funeral service going on. We went across the road to an old souvenir shop, and I bought a little copper pot. We went for a walk around the town. but a lot of the shops were shut. We think this is because the shopkeepers had gone to the funeral memorial service. We went back to the cathedral and everybody was coming out, so we went in and looked around.

We drove to St. Quentin and stopped so Mummy could go to the toilet. We went to the cathedral there then, and half of that had been destroyed in the Second World War. We left that cathedral then and drove on to Cambrai, and Jonny and Daddy went out and did some shopping. While they were gone it started to hail. From Cambrai, we drove on to a big town and then we drove on a motor way which we had to pay on and we drove to Clair Marais where we camped for the night. The lady went to a spot and we had to park there for the night. It was a hard standing which you had to drive over grass to get on to. What makes the matter worse is it had just been raining. We had our back tyre stuck in the mud and so the lady ran off. A lady came along and fetched her husband, another man came along and fetched his wife. All French. An English came along and another French, after about an hour, we got out. Then we went to bed after supper.

13th April 1983   Jon

We awoke at our campsite, did all the necessary things, collected everything together, lowered the roof and drove on to Calais.

We drove through Calais, viewed the supermarket but didn't stop. Then we drove to a beach and stopped.

Here Beth and I and Dad as well climbed up the sand dune and we found a German bunker of the Second World War and what we think is this is a gun emplacement. I started digging up the sand because I was curious.

We were called back to the van and had food. After this brief little interval we searched a different one and dug out a heap of sand in a hole in the wall.

After a while, we drove on past other bunkers up to Cap Blanc Nez. We looked at least five other bunkers. We drove on past lots of other bunkers including a round museum and an identical building which wasn't a museum.

Then we drove to Boulogne docks where Mum and Dad asked if going today was all right and Mum asked where the BEST hypermarket was. We drove around for ages trying to find out but eventually we found it. It was called Auchan.

In it were lots of little shops and a big Auchan supermarket. Beth, Dad and I did some shopping in a little shop then we all went round the big supermarket. We bought things and then went to a café where we bought tea. We drove to a dock and waited for the order to embark. When it finally came, we drove on.

During the voyage, Mum and I were up on deck most of the time.

When we came off, we went through customs with a funny man.

I slept in the van on the way to Grandma's at 2:00 A.M tomorrow.

Thanks to Nickson Kipkemoi for typing this up from the scans.

For any similar work, email: **kemboinic@gmail.com**

Interlude – Paris 1984

In the Easter holidays of 1984, I went again to Paris, this time with my secondary school. Whilst the details of this holiday are outside the scope of this book, the photographs I took survive, and the experience did relate importantly to my understanding both of France, for future of visits, and of the French language, such as that went.

There is no structure to hang the run of photographs on, because, whilst I remember we had a very difficult quiz to do in the coach as we went around Paris over the course of the week, I don't think any type of diary was attempted.

I have identified the locations of the vast majority of photographs using Google Lens, and friendly people on Twitter. Some things I photographed may have been by-the-by as the caught my interest, where-ever we were. A few remain unidentified for this reason.

We stayed at a hotel, somewhere in Paris, of which my main memories are the elevator shafts were taped-off gaping holes, and you had to use the stairs; that the corridor lights were on a timer and it took two of you to keep the light on long enough to unlock the doors; and that breakfast in a new outbuilding was fantastic, with the best hot chocolate I ever tasted, poured from large jugs.

The coach would pick us up and drive us around, but also we would use the Paris underground and quite often, at least, our day-time meals were in the same restaurant, where-ever it was, taking up several tables, whilst the rest of it was open to the public.

It was a very enjoyable holiday, for a large part due to a group of girls a year younger who were very friendly to us, and good company. Thanks, especially to Ali!

A photograph at the base of the Eiffel Tower, which was labelled in my old photo album as having some of our teachers in it, those in the foreground on the right. I really only remember Mr Gordon, head of department, who is not in the photo. The teachers are labelled in my atrocious handwriting as Mrs D-something, possibly Davies, Mrs Altor, if that is spelt right, and Mr Giles.

The 3 Andrews, with Daniel & Richard to the right, Kerry on the left

Les Invalides

Les Invalides – Approaching the tomb

Canons at Les Invalides – above inside, below outside

Church of the Dome of Les Invalides, which contains the tomb of Emperor Napoleon I, as well as his son, who died a teenager in Austria and never reigned, but was counted as Napoleon II.

The little Arc de Triomphe in Les Tuilleries

The Eiffel Tower as seen from the Avenue de Tourville

Tomb of the Unknown Soldier at the Arc de Triomphe

Sacre Coeur

The Chateau de l'Eau (water tower) near Sacre Coeur, Montmartre

Looking across Paris towards Notre Dame from the Sacre Coeur

The Louvre – this whole area is now pedestrianised

The Grand Palais from one of the Batoux Mouche boats upon the Seine, with the Pont Alexandre III in the foreground

The Pont Saint Martin from the Rue Saint Martin

Town Hall of the 5th Arrondissement

Part of the Fontaine Saint Michel

A griffin statue in front of the Fontaine Saint Michel

Rosalind photographing the Fontaine St Michel, behind her is a bridge, almost hidden in the perspective, with the building in the background on the other side of the river.

The Chapel of Saint Ursula, at the Sorbonne in the 5th Arrondissement. It has a famous crypt containing the body of Cardinal Richelieu, first minister under King Louis XIII in the 17th century. He was dug up and his face stolen during the French Revolution, but under Napoleon III his face was reinterred with his body. In 1895 it was exposed and photographed during repairs to the chapel.

The Palace at Fontainebleu

Fontainebleu

The palace at Compiegne, home to Napoleon III and Eugenie

Screen before the main courtyard at Compiegne, known as the Cour d'honneur and a place for parades and displays

Statue of Marshal Foch at Compiegne

I remember we visited the [replica] railway carriage at Compiegne, seeing the diorama of mannequins re-enacting the German signing of the Armistice in November 1918. I bought several postcards, including of the carriage and of the mannequins in the uniforms of various nationalities, including American and French soldiers of the First World War. If I still have these, I currently have no idea where they are.

The palace of Versailles

Versailles – round the back

Versailles – the door and emblem

An as -yet unidentified street in Paris, that must have appealed to me either for its absolute "Paris-ness" or because something of note was there…

In passing, I took a photo of the Moulin Rouge from the coach

A view down the Seine from a bridge

A car park with a nice statue

The Advantura

We bought the Advantura in late 1985. Dad and Beth journeyed down to Addiscombe in Croydon, South London to view it, and agreed to purchase it. For a while in early 1986 we had both motorhomes on the road. After that, the Buccaneer was parked up on the side lawn pending its sale, whilst the Advantura did all the business of being our motorhome.

The Advantura camper, on our driveway at home

Exciting for my sister and I, the Advantura initially came with a CB (Citizens' Band) radio and we could sit in it and call up other people, but we never knew what to say! The only thing that ever got an answer was "time check" where kind people would tell us what time it was. I did at some point make a list of the handles of local CB users. The radio set was above the front passenger drop-blind.

Inside the Advantura

My sister and I generally sat in the same places as in the Buccaneer, with me behind the passenger seat (Mum's) and she behind the driver's seat (Dad's). But because the Advantura had a permanent table and benches at the back (which converted into Mum and Dad's bed in the night) we would sometimes sit there, or lie down on the seats and either listen to music or sleep on the journey. Of course, sometimes I sat up front instead of Mum and helped Dad with the navigating.

My sister would sleep above the cab, just as in the Buccaneer, whilst I would sleep on a bed positioned across the two seats behind the front cab, or if time and weather allowed erect a tent adjacent to the camper and sleep in there. I remember sleeping in the camper, and needing the loo in the middle of the night, probably on the 1986 holiday, and sneaking out, so as not to wake anyone, across the predawn fields in the half-light, with the dew to the toilet block, and back.

The Advantura had speakers in the rear of the vehicle, so we could lay down there and listen to, e.g., David Bowie sing Changes or No More Heroes without having to be proximate to the cab where the cassette player was located.

Looking down the motorhome to
Beth sitting at the table at the back

Whilst the Advantura DID have a built-in toilet and shower, accessed by the door on the right above, we very rarely used it and instead would use the toilet blocks and showers provided by campsites.

France and Andorra 1986

Introduction

In July and August 1986, we set off in our Advantura camper van to France and Andorra on a 3-week long holiday, the longest we had ever had. I was 15, about to become 16 during the holiday. My sister Beth was 13 and a half. Mum and Dad were both still working, and indeed I was going to do 2 weeks work for my Dad in the warehouse he managed for Thomas Cook in Peterborough upon my return. Mum was a teacher on a supply basis.

This Travel Diary is taken from my diary, which I wrote in an exercise book, at least one page a day, sometimes two, from December 1985 up to January 1989. No days were ever omitted, though some days were full of waffle about whatever was on my mind. I have taken the salient parts, whilst keeping in other background matters that had some relevance or bearing upon the holiday, so as to bring the holiday better to life.

The photographs are a mixture of those I took myself, and those Dad took, plus postcards which I bought and glued into the diary from time-to-time. It was the only time I ever went down to the Pyrenees, though Mum and Dad would revisit a couple of decades later by doing the Pilgrim Road to Compostella.

The account begins in the days leading up to the holiday, with some thoughts, purchases, and some cakes all of which will be relevant during the holiday itself.

The Advantura at 2 Juniper Crescent

Tuesday July 8th 1986

We leave for France on Saturday.

It will be interesting to see all the things in France and Andorra, but I feel that perhaps I have too many holidays to appreciate them properly. I don't really like being parted from everything for periods of time - admittedly I can take things with me but my interests often change and it is difficult to compensate for this on holiday - and will be near impossible to do so in France because everything will be in French!

3 weeks is a long time to be away for.

I will get past some of this by sending postcards - all in all I will send postcards to:-

Louise and Ellis, Mari and Stephen, Andrew, Simon, Grandma, Grandad, Aunty Beryl and Uncle Dave, Uncle Colin and Aunty Mickie

A heck of a lot really, and will cost a lot. I will probably get financial aid for the family ones. I would also send Chris a postcard if I knew his address. I may also send my penfriend Remi Piala one. We'll see. That's all in the future.

After getting ready etc I iced my birthday cake with white, almond flavoured royal icing. Upon this I piped J and Hello in green icing of the same flavour (Hello because I couldn't think of what else to write). Put it in the fridge to allow icing to harden.

Cycled through Werrington and Walton to Lincoln Road and visited the antique/2nd hand bookshop there. For a total of £1 bought 3 books including Eagle Day (Battle of Britain) and one on African history.

Cycled over Rhubarb Bridge along Lincoln Road to town and went to the market where I bought 2 notebooks to use as diaries on holiday in France and Andorra,

Cycled along Cowgate and through Bus Station to Westgate and along Mayors Walk. Poured down here. Got drenched. Cycled home. It hadn't rained there! HUH!!

Beth made some little fruit cakes when she returned from school to use up my spare icing. I helped and then made tea of pizza etc.

Thursday 10th July 1986

The sending of postcards will be a useful distraction - God know what I'll put in them but I like writing to gather my thoughts or perhaps even to keep my brain alive,

Last night I sorted out some books to read while I am on holiday in France and Andorra. Usually I take only a couple and supplement this by buying new ones but in France the books, or at least most of the books, will be in French and I don't think having to translate everything I read will make the books very enjoyable, so I'm taking quite a few with me. These are:-

War of the Wingmen by Poul Anderson

Bought it on holiday (in Wales I think). Read it, very good. Taken only for back-up. NOTE - I got the name of the planet for my story from it, although I didn't realise it at the time... Diomeda

- The Gold of the Gods by Erich von Daniken

My only one of these I haven't read

- We Are Not The First by Andrew Thomas

Bought in Croydon recently. On same lines as Von Daniken's

- Jack of Eagles by James Blush

Science fiction (SF)

- The Legion of Space by Jack Williamson

SF

- Sub-Zero by Robert W. Walker

Sounds good. Similar disaster type to 'Ice Quake' and 'Deluge', both good books. About Chicago in a new Ice Age

- The Gods Themselves by Isaac Asimov

Unlikely to be that good because it is a race against time book and in such things they always win

- Perry Rhodan 14: Venus in Danger by Kurt Mahr

Sounds a bit of a weird book. Don't suppose it'll be that interesting

By Saturday many more may have been added - perhaps some history ones, or classics - To Kill a Mockingbird, perhaps, or Lorna Doon, or more like 1984. Our English teachers would like us to read more classics.

Tandy was limping from this morning so this evening Mum and Beth took her to the vet (Mr Smith). She had been bitten by another cat on her hind right leg. Also she had parasites in her ears. The vet gave her an injection for her leg wound and sprayed the parasites dead. She should be OK now.

The next book I will read is "The Legion of Space" by Jack Williamson. Hopefully it will be as good as "Time and Again" by Clifford D Simak which I finished today.

Friday 11th July 1986

Dubious weather with nice sunny spots

Last day before we go to France and Andorra

I washed and dressed, reading "The Legion of Space". Washed and dried up and then spent virtually the rest of the morning picking blackcurrants - at the end of the day we had 8 square pots full in the freezer, weighing over 5 lbs, plus a smaller one I'd done in the evening.

After a sandwich dinner, helped pack the camper with food and checked that all was there. Helping till before tea.

Afterwards finished 'The Legion of Space' lying on my bed listening to Meatloaf. The book was good; however it was flat occasionally and naiive and the fact that 4 heroes managed to come out of every danger alive and save mankind speaks for itself. However as an excuse it has that it was originally written in 1955. I think it would make a good film, if it hasn't already made one.

Saturday July 12th 1986

TODAY WE LEAVE FOR OUR SUMMER HOLIDAY IN FRANCE AND ANDORRA

LET'S HOPE MY 3 WEEK HOLIDAY WILL PROVE BENEFICIAL TO ME - MY BODY AND MY MIND

Today we didn't actually go abroad but whizzed (A-HEM!) down to Grandma's and spent the afternoon in Croydon and then travelled to Portsmouth and spent the night there.

Up c 1/2 7. Breakfast and washed and dressed., Final packing of the camper. Said goodbye to Tandy. Travelled down to London on a different quicker route, except that it wasn't, but it would have been had it not been for the huge 1/4 hour traffic jam at the entrance to the Dartford Tunnel. Arrived at Grandma's c 1pm.

Read "Perry Rhodan 14 - Venus in Danger". Dinner of potatoes, carrots, sweetcorn, Yorkshire pudding, beef, gravy and trifle, and then coffee.

Walked down to Safeways with Beth to get a few items of food. Beth had her shoes reheeled and soled. Returned to 56 Lynden Hyrst but people were not too pleased at our endeavours - we had bought too much milk and no sultana bran and Beth shouldn't have got her shoes re-soled.

Said and waved goodbye to Grandma and left c 1/2 8. Drove down to Portsmouth. We camped on the dockside queuing with other caravans. Played around with Beth. Had drink of hot chocolate - lovely. Made use of portacabins.

Tomorrow we get up at 6, wash and dress and join the queue for the Le Havre ferry which leaves at 1/2 8. I wonder what my holiday will be like. OK so far

Sunday 13th July 1986

Rather nice weather all day - smooth Channel crossing.

Woken up c 5am by an official who got us into the Le Havre lane. For a couple of hours we queued in various places for the ferry, whilst having breakfast.

The ferry we go on is called the Viking Valiant (Townsend Thoreson). To our left was the Viking Viscount (Townsend Thoreson). Both these ships sound familiar.

To our right was the Duc de Normandie (Brittany Ferries). Across the harbour - a few hundred yards - were warships, British probably destroyers or frigates. The number on the largest - most likely to be a destroyer - was 023. The others were in decreasing size 019 and 0108. To the left of the largest (023) was another warship that appeared to have a helicopter landing pad on the rear, but I couldn't see the rest of it for the Viking Viscount blocked the view. I could see very little of the 0108 because the Viking Valiant blocked the view.

The time is now 07:10 hours.

After finishing "Venus in Danger" I went for another survey of the ships in the harbour. To the right of the Duc de Normandie was another large one - the 012. I could see another warship across the harbour but couldn't make out its identification number. Behind the Duc de Normandie I think I spied another, but it could have been the bows of the 109 or 0108, since before I could only see their sterns. The large one to the left of the 023 could in fact be an aircraft carrier. The Duc de Normandie has already left now (it is 07:55 in English time, French time is an hour ahead of us so over there it is 08:55).

With the departure of the Viking Viscount I could see that the big ship to the left of the 023 was the L11

From on board the ferry we saw many more warships and forts.

The L11 is named the Intrepid and behind it over the jetty was the L10. To the right of the L10 was a small ship, number N38. Over the jetty behind the O (actually I think the O's were D's!) was the aircraft carrier Illustrious. The 019 (D19?) is the Glamorgan. The D12 was the Kent.

A Channel Islands ferry, the Corbiere (Nassau) docked to our right and to the left was the Sealink ferry Earl Granville. Two more warships far behind D12 (Kent). Some to left of these. Many ships moored in line astern of Illustrious - F60, F70. ?89, F12, M2807, D20 (Fife). Near Illustrious a few more - F70, D91, M166. The D108 was named the Cardiff.

On our way out we passed auxiliary A110 'Orangeleaf' and also an old wooden ship. Round forts in the harbour exit number 3 in total. Passed HMS Dolphin, a training centre, I suppose similar to the mothballed HMS Ganges from our Freston holiday.

Behind it I could see a black sub - probably preserved.

Uneventful ferry voyage. Read book 'Jack of Eagles' by James Blish - an OK book, not particularly thrilled me yet.

Arrived Le Havre 3:15 continental time; few ships to remark upon there.

We got totally lost trying to get out of Le Havre, mainly due to Dad not knowing the scale of the map he was using and presuming it to be much different from reality.

Drove down to Blangy le Chateau. First campsite we tried was full! Diverted to Domaine du Lac Good, very close to the village of Blangy le Chateau.

After tea of sandwiches etc and peaches and a couple of the little cakes made by Beth we went for a walk around the village - pretty and interesting.

After writing this bed soon after - before 11 for having an earlier night to compensate for recent late nights and early mornings.

Monday July 14th 1986

BASTILLE DAY in France - anniversary of the mobs storming of the Bastille Prison in (I think) 1789 which triggered off the French Revolution in which King Louis XVI was guillotined and also his wife Marie Antoinette.

Up c ¼ to 9. Had shower. Breakfast of cereal and fresh grapefruit juice. Washed and did dishes with a bit of assistance from Mum.

We left the campsite and drove the through the village of Blangy le Chateau to Lisieux and thence to Gacé with Mum navigating. At Gacé Mum and I swapped places and I navigated. Did rather well and never actually got lost. Despite my not wanting to stop for dinner till we reached our destination, Troo, we stopped before Vibrage in a lay-by because Mum was not feeling too good sitting in the back.

Sandwiches, bran cake and an orange for dinner. When we left, Mum and I swapped places and I had to navigate from behind - not very easy and thus we got lost twice. Finally arrived at Troo mid-afternoon.

Early this morning I got my birthday present from Mum and Dad early. It is a personal stereo with buttons on. I used it a few times today and wrote this listening to Meatloaf on it.

At Troo we visited the Troglodyte dwellings (cave houses) which were still in use at the beginning of this century. Visited a church there which, as far as I can gather, has 12th century bits in it.

Drove on, eventually reaching Vendome where, after a lengthy search we found the campsite we were after in the Rue Geoffrey

Martel (who I think was one of Napoleon's generals, but I am not sure).

Read on a chair outside the camper until tea after having helped Mum get it ready. Cooked tea of bacon, potatoes, sweetcorn plus peaches followed by bedtime cocoa.

Helped Beth wash up by carrying dishes and drying some. Cleaned teeth and refused permission to have a shower (I'll have one in the morning). Finished reading 'Jack of Eagles' - OK book - so started "Sub Zero". Promises to be good.

We could hear music just out of the campsite and could see a mass of people gathering. I left to find out what it was, followed by the rest of the family who I didn't see had followed me till afterwards. Listened to good French music on open air disco systems. Wandered around. Saw the very good looking French girl, and was standing behind her till quarter to 12 watching the Bastille Day fireworks display.

Left whilst U.S. song 'We Are The World' was playing. Bed tomorrow.

The camping at Vendôme - a very nice campsite where I had a nice time on Bastille Day.

Le Camping at Vendome, with the note from my Diary where it is glued in

Tuesday July 15th 1986

Very hot and sunny for most of the day, cooler later in the evening

Up c 1/2 past 9. Shower after normal type breakfast. After a read (Sub Zero by Robert W Walker, in my case) we went for a walk around the town - VENDOME

We visited the church - rather interesting, especially the war memorial of the 1870-71 Franco-Prussian War. NOTE - Geoffrey Martel was in fact an 11th century Count of Vendome who started the building of the abbey complex of which the church was a part.

We then walked up the very steep slopes to the castle which was shut - it must've been an almost impossible task to storm this stronghold. We viewed the town from an observation point and descended to the town. Mum bought some salami from a boucherie and some cakes from a patisserie. I bought a French newspaper, Le Parisien, from a shop.

We then returned to the camper where we had a sandwich dinner including some French bread bought yesterday. After reading "Sub Zero" I, under pressure, changed into my shorts and also put on my sleeveless t-shirt which I'd worn at Freston. Cleaned teeth and wrote this.

After finishing 'Sub Zero' I went into town on my own and looked around town. Bought 2 postcards but don't know who for yet. Returned to camper. Started writing a little story - SF basically. Tea later of meatballs, baked beans and Smash. Helped Mum with washing up.

Read "War of the Wingmen" by Poul Anderson.

Wednesday July 16th 1986

Another scorching hot day all-through

I wonder what today holds in store for me? I probably won't send any postcards till Friday (but then again you never know!). I'm not sure who I will send them to first - perhaps friends and Foresters.

The Bastille Day celebrations yesterday have strangely, I suppose, meant that I have a greater liking for the French people and feel much more friendly towards them.

Today apparently we shall all get up early - c 1/2 7 and Beth and I have to visit the ship at 8 to retrieve our ice pack. I hope to fit a shave in somewhere. God knows why we want to get up so early.

Up c8, showered, washed hair and breakfasted.

We left Vendome and drove to Chaumont whose chateau we intended to visit. It was shut from 11:25 to 13:30 and we were in that zone so would come back later. Bought 5 postcards, 3 of Chaumont Chateau and 2 of Loire Valley chateaus. Drove on to Montrichard where we did a lot of shopping for dinner.

Arrived at Chenonceau Chateau and had a dinner of sandwiches etc. We decided not to visit Chaumont but to go to Chenonceau instead - so thus I had 3 postcards of a chateau we didn't visit. Took 2 photos to empty film - one of the chateau, the other of a tower. We were going to the waxworks museum but would have had to pay extra, so we went back to the camper where we had drinks.

Writing a sort of autobiography.

Left soon after and drove non-stop for ages out of the Loire area to the town of Bellac (pronounced Belloc), South-East of Poitiers. Wrote postcards to Andrew, Simon, Chris, Grandad, and Auntie Beryl and Uncle Dave.

Dad blew the electrics

Bed late for we arrived late.

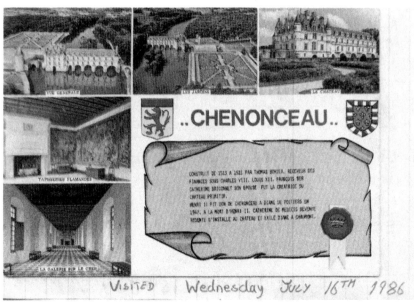

Photograph of Chenonceau, above, & postcard of the chateau below

Thursday July 17th 1986

Another hot, scorching day

I am still intending to send postcards to Mari and Stephen, Louise and Ellis, and the Inghams. I also intend to send postcards to Uncle Colin & Aunty Mickie, and to Grandma (from Andorra) and may even send my pen friend one.

An important thing I forgot to mention yesterday - whilst plugging our camper into an electrics point on the campsite at Bellac, Dad succeeded in blowing the system and cutting off several French campers who crowded round our van none too pleased. We were helped by our neighbour, a Scot, who translated. Eventually an electrician fixed the power point - by then the French had re-connected elsewhere, using extension leads. We decided we dared not risk attaching ourselves again.

Also, yesterday I got given by Mum my birthday present from Uncle Colin and family. It is a little electronic machine for working out the rate of exchange and various prices between countries - e.g. at present 11 Francs to the pound, so could work out for example what 6 Francs would be in Sterling. But it didn't work and despite taking it to an electrician/technician in Limoges it still doesn't work properly.

Up earliesh. As usual had a shower. In bed, first thing, I take off my pyjama trousers (I don't wear a top) and replace it with shorts - no underwear yet. I get out o bed, put on a t-shirt and shoes and go for a shower, carrying a bag with underwear in which I put on after the shower.

After breakfast wrote a postcard - in ENGLISH - to my so-called penfriend, Remi Piola from near Paris.

First today we drove to Oradour sur Glane and visited the ruined village there - destroyed by Germans in 1944 and its population massacred in reprisal for some French Resistance action or other. After a little wander around the modern village afterwards, we drove to the city of Limoges. Here I bought 6 stamps which I affixed to my postcards. Walked around the town getting very hot and thirsty.

Sandwich type dinner here before we drove off in late early-afternoon. Drove the 70 or so miles South to Perigeux where we arrived at a good campsite. But the damn place was full so we had to leave! The site we are on now is not at all that good in my opinion.

Started writing a little story set in the near future in which a sleek black and gold Citroen estate has a prominent part.

Postcards posted today. Finished "War of the Wingmen" - very good book. Will next read "King and Joker" by Peter Dickinson.

Bed late after a cooked tea.

Postcard of Barnabé Plage, Perigeux

Barnabe Plage, Perigeux, my sister and my Dad, who had been there decades before

Friday July 18th 1986

Still have 2 postcards but at present not in the mood for writing them so they'll have to wait

I'm heading towards being a walking bandage by the end of the holiday - at Vendome I gained a rather bad graze on my right angle and since then it has worn a plaster which has been changed once since - at Bellac - but will also be changed tomorrow.

I have something like athletes foot between my littlest toes of my right foot and they had a plaster but I replaced it with a bit of toilet paper for it was very uncomfortable.

I gained a scattering of splinters in a finger at Oradour which have still to come out.

This evening I fell off a rope-swing at this campsite at ALBIAS and gained a rope-burn/cut to the index finger of my left hand, which has since had a plaster applied, and a minor rope burn to my left foot which needed no attention, and a rather painful rope burn on my upper left arm to which I applied Savlon antiseptic spray but no plaster.

The most painful of these was the one between my toes, but in going for a swim this evening - I did not want to because of my injuries to my right foot, but was ordered to - the right ankle has become very painful. I applied more antiseptic to it but kept the same plaster, for Mum was becoming annoyed at the amount of plasters I use. It stung like mad and now hurts more. God knows when I will be able to go to sleep.

We were up earliesh by camping standards and had a shower. Started reading Beth's library book 'King and Joker' by Peter Dickinson. After breakfast we went for a little walk, crossing the river on a rope-pulled boat. I wandered around the streets of Trelissac and returned to find parents angry at my disappearance. Bought 2 postcards of the campsite for 1.75 Francs each! After Beth and Dad had gone for a swim we left c Midday.

We drove South to Les Eyzies, getting lost enroute of course. We got lost yesterday looking for the first campsite - I navigating said "Turn", they wouldn't but should have.

At Les Eyzies we visited some rather interesting caves - Le Grotto Grande Roc (or something). The guide gave us English people an English commentary.

After a sandwich dinner in the car park , reading "King and Joker" - rather good book - we drove on South relentlessly, finally arriving at the campsite at Albias, 50km North of Toulouse, in the early evening.

A play area here - when I went I got spoken to by 3 French kids, 2 young boys and a little girl. Couldn't understand them.

Reading then tea of meatballs etc. Washing up with Beth.

Bed c11.

Saturday 19th July 1986

Weather warmish but with a coolish breeze

Last night wrote a postcard to Mari and Stephen showing the campsite of the 17/18 July. Will send when bought stamps. Still got postcards to send to: Grandma, Uncle Colin and family, the Inghams, Louise and Ellis. Have to buy them plus stamps.

Up c9ish. Spent all morning on the campsite. Got washed and dressed - no shower for it aggravates my wounds, water does. In spite of the pain last night and rather painful itch I did manage to get to sleep pretty quickly listening to Meatloaf on my personal stereo.

Did washing up on my own. Read 'King and Joker' till we left after Midday.

Drove South to Montauban then East to Albi where I took a photo across the river. Had dinner of French bread and things on it in a layby outside Albi.

Drove through Castres, South to Mazaret* where we stopped in the Black Mountains to view the gorge valley and take a photo. We then drove to Carcassonne. The first campsite we went to - in the city centre - we did not like, so we left the city and drove to another at Lavandieres.

Visited village where bought a cornetto. Beth bought one too with my money, and Mum and Dad did shopping with more of it so I am owed 5 Francs by Beth and 50 Francs by Mum and Dad. Returned to the van and laid the table.

Reading till tea and finished the book - rather good. Tea of ravioli etc. Did washing and drying on my own.

Started devizing a story (YES another one!) set in 2082 and featuring the world after a war, and a future British royal family under King James III. Drew out family trees for it - took most of the night until c 1/2 10.

Dad was showing another Briton around our camper.

Sent postcard to Mari and Stephen. Bed after 11

* Both my diary and Dad's logbook has this as Mazaret, but looking it up it seems more likely to be Mazamet

My photograph of Albi

Sunday 20th July 1986

This campsite is nice and not too noisy, if slightly overcrowded.

Up c8. Shower. Did dishes. Soon we left and drove to the old part of Carcassonne. We spent an enjoyable morning here, walking on old defences and up narrow streets. I took numerous photos, bought half a dozen postcards and a book about the city - in English - for the equivalent of £1.54 (17 Francs). Visited the cathedral of St. Nazaire there but couldn't find any of the things of interest listed in my book about it.

Returned to the camper in the car park just outside the old cite, for a dinner of French bread and things on it, a bran cake and a peach.

Writing my story set in 2082 where the major countries in the world are European, after the nuclear war of 2003. There have been wars after that - the longest and most recent being the war of 2077-80 during which the Belgian Battlefleet sailed up the Thames in 2079 and spent 2 days bombarding London, during which St Pauls, Westminster Abbey, Buckingham Palace and Westminster Palace (in our reality the Houses of Parliament, but it was in use as a palace) had been destroyed & 2 heirs to the throne killed.

I dried up after Mum had washed the dishes. Dad and Beth went back into the old city where Beth bought a fan and Dad a bottle of wine.

Thence onwards, we drove South into the Pyrenees and all the way to the large town of Ax Les Thermes where we went to the campsite nearby at the village of Orlu. Enroute we stopped twice and I took photos of the view.

The campsite is good, slightly crowded but not too much. All nationalities here, including Irish. Went for a walk around the village and returned with Beth along the river. During the rest of the evening, Dad and Mum were talking to our French neighbours who has a young daughter of 10 or so called Selene and a 3 year old white rabbit on a leash.

Wrote story before bed c 11.

The city of CARCASSONNE which was a major factor in my t, is here but not the only one

Postcards of Carcassonne

Carcassonne, above a photo by me, and below a photo by Dad

Another view of the walls of Carcassonne (above) & (below) by the Orlu campsite at Ax-les-Thermes

Near the campsite

Monday 21st July 1986

Wrote the postcard last night for Louise and Ellis, will post when I can buy stamps, hopefully tomorrow, probably from Andorra.

The French family next to us consists of a man aged c50 - the main participant in Mum and Dad's hours-long conversation with them last night - his wife, their 2 daughters (Selena aged around 11, and an older girl called either Natalie or Catherine aged 15 or so, and a friend who had the other name). Also they had a 3-year old white rabbit kept on a leash which was tied to something inside the tent, and whose name was a repetition of some syllables twice, Zaza or Lulu - if anything it was nearer the first (zar-zar?) than the second. They had a dog also but had not brought it with them. They are to be at that campsite for a total of 2 weeks.

Woken in the night c 1/4 to 3 and visited the toilet block. It was ruddy freezing! Woken by Dad before 9 after being very cold for the rest of the night. Had a shower, cornflakes and a round of toast (I don't usually have that for breakfast but did today, because of the cold - due to us being in a mountain valley, where the sun takes longer to reach us)

Had a shave with my Bic - my Braun electric one won't fit the razor fittings on the continent. We left after 10, after I had written a bit more of my story.

Drove through mountain roads until we hit a huge traffic jam at the frontier town of Pas de la Casa. Strange that when we arrived there we were waved straight through and hardly stopped, so little obvious reason for the traffic jam which ended at the customs point.

Drove up out of the town and stopped above it for dinner. Wrote a bit more of my story. Dinner of 3 rounds of near-mouldy thick brown bread brought from home and 2 pieces of French bread with peanut butter, yeast extract and French cheese portions on. Plus a nectarine.

Took a photo of two horses, one a foal, that had ventured into the car park. Then we drove on to the town of Canillo.

Bought 4 postcards here of Andorra for the amazingly cheap price of half a France each, about 4½ pence. Andorra accepts both French Francs and Spanish Pesetas and has no currency of its own, unlike Luxembourg for instance, which I visited last year on the way to Switzerland with the school.

Drove on to and through Andorra la Vella - meaning Andorra the Old, I believe.

At campsite in the suburbs of the city called Riberaygua - an OK place. Upon arriving Dad and Beth went swimming. I tried to write more of my story but the wind blew everything away so I gave up in annoyance.

Walked around campsite but not very interesting. Later on the family next to us returned, a Spanish one.

Tea of meatballs etc. After tea went for a boring walk through the town, boring because of the slow speed and the aimlessness of it. After returning I wrote postcards for the Inghams, Grandma, Uncle Colin etc. Then to bed

Pas de la Casa – you can see the top of the advantura in the middle row of vehicles

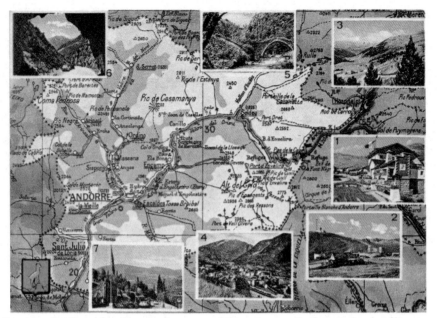

Postcards bought in Andorra, with maps of the Principality on themselves

Tuesday 22nd July 1986

Not a bad start, hot day, cool evening and some rain

It's funny I just realised it's my birthday tomorrow. Have still to post Louise & Ellis's postcard as well as the 3 I wrote last night.

My first impressions of Andorra are not too good. The towns are rather ugly and very busy with vehicles meaning that they smell of exhaust fumes. The scenery is striking, mainly villages and mountains. I'm still to find something that really interests me, perhaps tomorrow, else I'd have preferred to be in FRANCE.

Woken up by Dad. Went for a shower after a glass of apple juice. Was going to wash my hair but the shower was coolish and very fast and splashed everywhere so I came out quickly.

Left campsite and drove Southwards out of Andorra la Vella to and through the town of San Julia to the Spanish border. Turned around and went up mountainish to La Massana and up mountain towards Pal. Saw campsite - Xixarella - and visited it. Decided to stay.

The place we first tried to stop had a French family next to us, but was not level enough and we crossed the road to another place, but still not level. Crossed back over to be behind the French family.

Had dinner of French bread, 1/2 a blackcurrant tart, 1/2 orange and chufa (a sort of almondy milk drink which I think is very nice though Beth does not like it). Went for a small walk round the campsite - no British, but one did come later; I heard British voices while in the toilets later, and Mum and Beth verify this.

Playing in the stream whilst the others went for a swim. They tried to drag me along but I refused, as much because of aggravation caused to my ankle wound last time as for the fact that sitting in a pool of freezing water, or even swimming up and down in it, is not really exactly thrilling. Dammed part of the mini-river near us instead.

We were going to play mini golf, but too expensive. Spent all of the rest of the afternoon/early evening up till tea at c8pm, I believe, writing a long chapter of my 2082 story - war has been declared between France and Britain.

Cookedish tea. 'ish' because of cold meat. Chocolate yoghurt. Wash up with Beth, I drying. We made beds. Washed and toileted. Wrote this. Bed after 111.

Xixarella Campsite, from a postcard

Xixarella campsite, my sister and Mum by the van, above

The campsite at Xixarella, showing our camper lower right

Wednesday July 23rd 1986

Coolish start, normal hot day, cool evening

GOOD GOD! IT'S MY BIRTHDAY

It doesn't mean that much to me, now and where we are, but it'll mean we can have some of my birthday cake.

Already had some presents - personal stereo from Mum and Dad (very useful - use it quite often, hope batteries won't run out) and the exchange thing from Uncle Colin and family - Dad finally got it working last night. It will come in useful for Mum's shopping but I can do most calculations in my head fast enough. Wonder what Beth'll give me as a present - she bought it outside the chateau of Chaumont which we didn't visit - thus meaning I'd bought 3 postcards of somewhere we didn't go - I sent these to my friends (Andrew, Simon and Chris)

ROYAL WEDDING OF PRINCE ANDREW AND SARAH FERGUSON

Haven't heard or seen any international news for ages so God knows what is going on in the world. I'll have a look at a newspaper in a shop. Must get stamps for the postcards too!

This is in fact a rather nice campsite and much better than the one of 21/22 July.

Up c 1/2 8. Made breakfasts - for once I had a new cereal bought yesterday at Jumbo hyper-market near San Julia. it was very nice, tasting of apricots mainly. Washed and toileted.

PRESENTS plus CARDS. From Beth I got a flick comb (called for some reason a cow comb). From Grandma I got 180 Frances - over £17!

Bought 2 postcards from the campsite, one stuck into the diary (above).

Drove on down to La Massana where I bought a French newspaper - Le Figaro. I had been intending to buy an Andorran one but there aren't any. Bought history magazine/book about WW2 secret services, in French for 25 Francs. Part of presents from Grandma thus.

Went out for dinner at MARCO POLO RESTAURANT where there was a Scottish waiter. Had garlic chicken and chips plus cake. Went for a little drive up to Ordino and back to La Massana where I bought 5 Andorran stamps for postcards which I at last sent. Bought 3 more postcards of Andorra.

Drove off through Esclades and Encamp to Catholic sanctuary of Meritxell. Very nice place - liked it for its possible potential as a fort, strangely enough. Took 6 photos of it and bought 2 postcards.

Drove on to Pas de la Casa - frontier town - where Mum and Dad bought alcohol whilst Beth and I made a birthday tea consisting of bread and birthday cake -yummy! Ate it.

We decided to camp on the car park, many others doing so.

A bit sad, because if we hadn't we would have gone to Orlu and met up with Selena and family again.

On my sixteenth birthday, with Beth, up past Ordino, Andorra

Dad, up past Ordino, Andorra, and (below) the ski run down from there, seen in Summer

In the Winter this is a ski slope

The old sanctuary at Meritxell, which had burned down and been replaced with the new one

Slightly crazy angle of the new sanctuary at Meritxell, and, below, inside it

VISITED Wednesday July 23RD 1986

Postcard of the old sanctuary of Meritxell (above) and the new sanctuary (below)

OLD →

VISITED 23rd July (My 16TH Birthday) 1986

Another view of the interior of the new sanctuary at Meritxell

Thursday July 24th 1986

Cold start. Not sunny today. Warmed up later.

WE GO BACK INTO FRANCE TODAY. At present encamped in car park near customs to France. Funny old place!

Up 8ish. Sort of washed and dressed in camper. We then went round the town which is full of shops - mainly supermarkets and mini hypermarkets. All in all I bought:-

- 3 C60 (hour long) cassettes = 9 Francs

- Box of Airfix HO/OO scale astronauts = 7 Francs

- Revel 1/72 Scale Heinkel 162 = 11 Francs

- Tight Fit cassette including The Lion Sleeps Tonight = 11 Francs

- Postcard with a map of Andorra

- and a free Andorran newspaper - well, they do have them, but only free!

Drove on after half past 11. Passed customs without need to stop. Drove into France past huge traffic jam queuing to get into Andorra, and through fog (actually a low cloud). Sadly didn't go back to Ax Les Thermes and Orlu campsite with Selena's family.

Drove West. Stopped at castle town of Foix for dinner. Assembled my 14 astronauts and their equipment.

Drove on to a campsite eventually, after 5 near Saint Gaudens.

Rather nice place. Rather deserted - i.e. not many other occupants. Owner is a woman.

In the afternoon devised a game out of Beth's Tarot cards that she bought for 22 Francs at Pas de la Casa this morning. Nothing about fortune telling in the instructions which give rules of a game in French, so very difficult to understand. Named the game I invented, 'Heron'. Cards have 4 sets of Hearts, Clubs, Diamonds, Spades with 1 to 10, V (= Jack on English), D (= Queen), R (=King) and a C for Cavalier. Also 1 to 21 of cards with pictures on plus a Joker and a Heron card which I think is only the title card, for it is the make of the cards, but I included it in the game. Game complicated at first, but easy to get hang of, and gets easier as it progresses.

Wrote 4 pages of instructions bought today at a French supermarket where Beth got some more batteries for her personal stereo. Playing the game - for 2 players only - outside the van on the big table.

Tea of real sausages, tinned potatoes and baked beans plus tinned apricots with cake. No birthday cake today. Went for shower but the lady was just locking up, so washed all over whilst the toilets were empty. Made the beds. Played game of 'Heron' with Beth - she kept winning! Wrote this listening to Tight Fit on my personal stereo.

Friday 25th July 1986

When I get back I'll be working for a fortnight somewhere in Thomas Cook - getting paid. I hope I don't have to wear a suit and all that, then I may enjoy myself!

Up c 1/2 8. Shower and washed

We drove into Saint Gaudens. War memorial there commemorating Pyrenean French military leaders - Foch, Joffre, Gallieni of World War One, Soult, Murat, Bernadotte, Bessiers, of Napoleon's marshals.

Walked around the town looking for a model shop where I could buy glue so as to be able to assemble the He 162 if I feel like it - I have done things like this before, building a Me 262 in Wales, and a Stug III in Wales. No glue found. Bought a French History magazine from a shop - cost 13 Francs, covering the first years of the Thirty Years War, and French involvement in it under Richelieu.

Took a photo of the monument of WW1 marshals.

Drove out and on to St Bertrand de Comminges. Visited a Roman church there, but it closed. Walked up to the cathedral (Romanesque/Gothic style) in the newer area of town on a hill, but it had just closed. Walked around and back to the camper. Got dinner ready. Saw a rat! Had French bread dinner and birthday cake.

Drove hence to Arreau and then over valleys etc. Good campsite - L'Oree Des Monts at La Seoube in Haute-Pyrenees. In trees, with a shower and hot water in the wash basins. Bought a postcard of it. Got tea ready - Spanish ravioli and peas. Apricots (tinned). A couple of nice Spanish milk biscuits and evaporated milk. Supper of Spanish chocolate milk - very nice - and a couple of crocettes - similar to Krispen. Washed up in outdoor sinks opposite our camper parked in the tree'd area.

Afterwards played Heron, all 4 of us. I won (had played one this morning with Beth and again she won). Listening to Nik Kershaw's Human Racing cassette whilst playing - enjoyable. It was the first cassette Beth had of him, bought Christmas 1984 by Mum and Dad for her. She's a Nik Kershaw and A-ha fan and has both of Nik Kershaw's cassettes and A-ha's Hunting High and Low. Afterwards played 12 games of Speed. In all Mum was the winner with less points though Dad won most games.

Washed and brushed teeth. Helped make beds. Wrote most of this listening to the first side of Nik Kershaw's Human Racing. Batteries of personal stereo failing and playing slow now. Bed c11.

L'Oree Des Monts at La Seoube

Saturday July 26th 1986

Rainy start, cool all day

Up after half past 8. Washed and dressed - actually the other way round, by necessity: up, dressed in van, washed in toilet block, back to van.

Breakfast of my Spanish cereal and a round of toast and yeast extract.

Left the campsite after half past 10, after reading 'Short History of Africa' - the section on the colonial period.

Drove to LOURDES eventually - the religious place, because in 1838 the Virgin Mary is supposed to have appeared to a terminally ill young lady called Bernadette and told her how to cure herself. Since then a big church and other strange religious buildings plus a small park and a large underground cavern for services have sprung up around it. Dying people or people with serious illnesses come to Lourdes in the hope of being cured. Many thousands more so-called pilgrims, plus probably only visitors like us, come to see the place.

It's sort of impressive but heavily commercialised with stalls selling the candles Catholics are so fond of lighting, with the two main streets leading down to the one literally full of souvenir shops - many tens of them, all selling virtually the same thing at around the same price. I bought a couple of little charms/trinkets because they looked nice (one blue, and one gold) and 3 glass/pottery figures because they'd look good on my shelves.

The religious area was swarming with people from all over Europe - Britain, Italy, Spain - and many ill people in wheelchairs and even beds. In certain areas people were queuing to touch a religious cave wall or wash their face with water. All rather queer.

We drove out of Lourdes to the campsite pictured (Camping Arc-en-Ciel). Tea of sausage, croquet potatoes and yoghurt. Washed dishes. Started a new book, 'Wolf' by Leo Kessler. Game of Keyword before bed.

Camping Arc-en-Ciel, with contemporary notes from my Diary

Two of the little statues of the Madonna, purchased at Lourdes

Sunday 27th July 1986

Cool start, warmish afternoon, average evening.

Up before 9 after having visited the toilets at 6am. It was rather nice at that time of the day. Surprisingly I didn't wake anybody up, either leaving the can or getting back into bed; which is especially in Mum's case for usually any noise wakes her.

After a breakfast of tinned grapefruit and toast (2 rounds, 1 with yeast extract, the other with nothing at all) I helped Dad do the dishes.

Did part of my model aircraft bought at Pas-de-la-Casa and assembled in the main yesterday - IT ISN'T A HEINKEL 162 although it says it is on the box. It was obviously packed incorrectly at the factory for it has the cellophane on still. It is in fact a FOCKE WULF 190 - still German, so it's OK. I've already got one of these hanging on my ceiling, but wargames have taken their toll of it; it has lost its landing gear, and its propellers - decimated - have been replaced by a disc of clear plastic to represent spinning propellers, so it looks quite convincing as if flying. I prefer to get German models as a result of the wargames of the 2nd to 4th Years where I almost always played the Germans. Since then in all HISTORICAL games etc I have preferred to be the side that actually lost the war - i.e. Germans in WW2, French Napoleonic.

Back to today! We left the campsite and drove on West of Lourdes to some caves which promised to be very interesting - a cable car trip followed by a boat trip and a train journey underground in the caves. Unfortunately the price was 28 Francs each (equal to £2.58) and we only had a total of 120 Francs. This would have left us with hardly any money for the rest of the day. After deliberation, Dad and Beth went, while Mum and I returned to the camper.

I read 'Wolf' till they returned c 1pm. I made dinner and gave it to them: French bread, my birthday cake and a peach. Afterwards we drove off. We drove along small country roads, getting lost a couple of times, ending at a quarry once, and a farm another time. Eventually we found the right road to Col de Souter - funny place, with a strange old antique/junk shop at the top. Moved on, along very dangerous narrow roads on the side of the mountain, sometimes with cows or goats in the way on the road, to Col d'Aubisque.

Thence we drove on down the mountain to the valley floor where we eventually found a campsite. Pulled in - MON PLAISIR. OK place, I suppose, though once I'd finished 'Wolf' - a good book - I was dead bored for a while. Did as much towards tea as I could.

Started writing another story involving Seb, Chris, Nichola. Tea of scrambled egg, croquet potatoes, sweet corn and rice pudding.

Wrote this listening to Nik Kershaw's "The Riddle' cassette off Beth. Made the beds.

Monday July 28th 1986

Very hot, and warm & sweaty in the main

Up after 9. Shower and then breakfast of prunes and French bread. Listened to Nik Kershaw's 'Human Racing' cassette.

Drove off at quarter past 10. We drove to Pau looking for a bank to cash travellers' cheques as we are out of money. None!

Drove to a place beginning with O. Had dinner of French bread etc, half of a cake bought at the campsite near Lourdes, and a plum. Looking for a bank but none again.

Drove to Dax looking for a bank, whilst I searched for a model shop. I found a toy shop with models, but bad prices for glue and paint - 50p dearer than back home. No bank found.

Had to use my 100 France note when we eventually found a campsite.

Reading 'Battle for St. Lo' by a Major Johns who was there - interesting.

Helped make tea with Beth - a splodge of pate, sweetcorn, tinned potatoes and some tinned fruit.

WE HAVE A FLAT TYRE! Mum and Dad went off to make an expensive phone call to get insurers to help. Beth and I had a bowl of cornflakes with chocolate custard. I washed and dried up. Listening to Nik Kershaw's 'Human Racing'.

Played a long game of Heron

From Dad's Logbook

Phoned Europe Assistance from public call box - This cost in total 12 Francs. Gave reference number - woman asked if I had called before - if not, where did I get reference number from, where had I bought the insurance? What was the reference number of the seller? Eventually and after a rephone, asked the same set of questions, then asked for phone number to phone back. Not quite enough time as the number was on the outside of the box. Cut off again around 8pm. Walked back to the site and asked the warden to use his phone. Got a different woman who asked for a number to phone back on – cost another 12 Francs.

Then phoned by a man who took all the details of insurance, vehicle, me etc. Said he would try to get someone out. If not, he would ring back. He did, at 11pm. He left a message that a garage at Bayonne would be on site at 8:30am. Phone call from garage asking size of tyre. Explained that we wanted the wheel changed. Said he would be there at 10am. Arrived at 10:45.

Tuesday July 29th 1986

Cool start. Warmish afternoon. Nice evening.

A week hence we'll be back in ENGLAND.

Up 7 for we thought we'd all better be ready by half 8 when the man from the garage would come. Made breakfast - prunes and French bread. Shower. Read 'Battle for St. Lo' by Glover S. Johns Jr. until the man from the garage had come at around half 10. He replaced the flat tyre with our spare one which Dad couldn't do because he didn't have a big enough jack, and he didn't know how to, having only changed the wheel on a car before.

We left around quarter to 12. Straight after, the hub cap fell off the new wheel and part of it got run over. Dad pulled up and retrieved it to put it back on later. We drove to the seaside at Seignose and finally caught a bank that was open - apparently banks don't open on a Monday anymore.

Did shopping in a supermarket. Returned to the camper. Made dinner - French bread etc plus yeast extract, chocolate spread, cheese spread, Bonbel cheese. Had the last of my birthday cake and an orange.

Walked to the beach. During the course of our stay there I built a large sand castle/city c 6 metres square at least. A nice French girl built one near me.

Reading 'Battle for St. Lo' c. quarter to 4.

As we left the car park, the hub cap fell off again, and Dad pulled up and retrieved it again. As yet, as I write this, he has not replaced it.

He may in fact not bother since all it seems to want to do is to fall off.

Drove North up the coast. Missed a turning so headed inland. Finally arrived at a good cheap campsite at a place called Bilos near Salles. We will visit either the nearby town beginning with A or Bordeaux tomorrow. Many British people here - at least 4 others out of about 15 units. Of the rest, some at least are Dutch and I wouldn't be surprised to see a German.

Helped Mum make tea of nice sausages, tinned new potatoes and tinned carrots, followed by a strawberry or raspberry yoghurt, all bought this morning at the supermarket.

Finally got the money I was owed back.

Did dishes. Read. Wrote. Made the beds. Rest. Wrote this.

Wednesday July 30th 1986

Hot day, after average start with thunder and rain late afternoon

I wonder what today will bring? No doubt we'll get lost again as usual and all that entails BUT I'm thinking more along the lines of personal enjoyment - will the A place provide any?

Up c 20 to 9. Helped make breakfasts - cereal for first time in ages - cornflakes, and 2 rounds of the tiny toast which I did under the grill. Good wash. Reading 'Battle for St. Lo'.

Good start - went wrong way out of campsite so were lost straight away! Turned around and found correct road. Drove to Biscarrosse. Looked at a few shops. Looking for German models. Found some tanks and half-tracks but too damn expensive - twice the cost as they would be back home, so no point buying them. Also there were some Atlantic figures at a reasonable price, but this make is too large to be HO scale (1/72).

Drove to beach. Lay on towel reading 'Battle for St. Lo'. Sand too dry to build with and beach really too crowded. Mum sunbathed. Dad and Beth swam in the sea.

Left after an hour and drove to the woods. Made dinner of French bread etc, orange. Dried dishes. Drove off to the Dune de Pyla (Pilat) - highest sand dune in Europe, at 130 metres I think. Climbed to the top up the steps. Ran across the dune to a tilted German bunker. Interesting but the run there was exhausting and I was dizzy walking inside at a crazy angle. Damned difficult to climb back up the dune!

Drove to Arcachon and visited Mammouth hyper-market. Got lost looking for campsite, but finally found it - the municipal. OK place. Rather full. A couple of other Brits - as usual Dad struck up a conversation with one, a young man from Cornwall with a Commer motorhome.

Made tea of sausages and beans etc from a tin and French mashed potato from a packet - Mousline. French Angel Delight sort of thing.

Had a shower. Finished 'Battle For St. Lo' - a good book, interesting and learnt a lot.

Got beds ready whilst Mum and Dad did dishes for once. Toilet and cleaned teeth. Bed late around half past 11.

Thursday 31st July 1986

Rainy start, overcast the rest of the day

The days creep on towards home-going time. Of our time left in France, I'm most looking forward to our visit to Normandy and the Second World War connection. Unfortunately, when we left home I didn't know I would be interested in the Second World War and accordingly didn't bring any reading material on it, save 'The Battle for St. Lo', which I hadn't intended to read, just to use as a guide if we went to St. Lo - I had once started reading the book, probably in 2nd Year form time, but had got no further than page 15. If I had known my interests would be thus, I have many other books I would have liked to read - 'Rise and Fall of the Third Reich', 'Ardennes Offensive', 'Hitler's War on Russia', my newest from Castor and perhaps even a 'A Bridge To Far' by Cornelius Ryan again - I first read it in 2nd Year form times; I can remember it rather clearly. Ah well...

Up c half 7 to have a shower and wash hair. Had a shower but didn't wash hair for the shower was cold. Breakfast of weetabix and cornflakes and two rounds of tiny toast with yeast extract on.

Drove to Bordeaux where I searched everywhere for a shop selling models but found none; this was in a sort of outer central area. We didn't go to the centre. Mum and Dad changed some travellers' cheques. Traffic jam getting out due to an accident between a white Peugeot van and a red Porsche sports car.

Drove North to Angouleme. Stopped in a rest area for dinner of French bread with ham - not too nice, but OK I suppose with yeast extract, and Bonbel cheese (very nice). An orange and a couple of biscuits for dessert.

Reading 'Passenger to Frankfurt' by Agatha Christie - started it this morning; quite interesting.

Drove on past Poitiers. Went to a Carrefoure hypermarket. Beth and I had great difficulty getting our deposit back on bottles and buying some lemonade. We managed it eventually.

Drove to Richelieu - I think, anyhow. In a shop there found some models. The aircraft included a Heinkel 162, which was rather expensive. Also ESCI infantry at 15 Francs, which was rather expensive. The only Germans they had were Afrika Korps, but I bought a packet/box of 50. Spent most of the rest of the day making them appear to be normal soldiers and altering positions of a few.

Drove to a campsite nearby. Many British here, a Dutch, a German and some French. Quite nice, but I feel a rather hostile French family on site.

Friday August 1st 1986

Hottish after a cool start

Last night put new batteries in my personal stereo and wrote my diary listening to Meatloaf - very good after not having heard him for a week or so, not since Andorra La Vella, I think.

Up c8 am. Had shower and washed hair. Had to obtain a token to be able to get hot water for a shower. Cost 2 and a half Francs, about 25p. Mum paid. The campsite price was very good, so this was little loss.

Breakfast of weetabix and cornflakes, and a sprinkling of rice krispies, plus 2 rounds of almost normal-sized toast with yeast extract. Wrote another postcard to Grandma, thanking her for my birthday money. Posted it in Richelieu when we passed through.

Drove to Chinon, where there is a big chateau of historical importance, but we didn't visit it. Walked around the shopping area. Bought a pack of 50 ESCI German infantry for 12 and a half Francs.

Drove to an abbey where Richard I of England and Henry II of England were originally buried - [FONTEVRAUD ABBEY]

Rather expensive for adults to go in. Beth and I could have gone for 3 Francs each, but after some thought declined. I bought a large poster showing the royal lines of Britain and France. Very interesting - for instance, France should have a King Henry at present if it were not a republic. Bloody expensive at 40 Francs but in my opinion worth it.

Made dinner of French bread etc plus an orange. Reading 'A Passenger to Frankfurt' - OK book, but not as Beth said it would be.

With my present interest in WW2 I only read it because Beth said it was about the Hitler Youth. It is not. It is set in 1970 and involves the youth of then.

Travelling all afternoon, through Saumur and Angers. Here I lay down and listened to Meatloaf on my personal stereo, trying to get to sleep - managed it for 1 minute in the middle of Paradise by the Dashboard Light.

When I got up we were in Laval. We drove to Drassy - something like that* - after getting lost. Had mug of tea. Read, and toileted in public loos.

Drove to a campsite to the South (I think) of Flers. Conde sur Noireau (means Conde on Blackwater).

Bored for a lot of the evening. Book rather unexciting, though OK. Washed and dried up. Made own bed. Studied the family tree poster of kings. Bed.

*Dad's logbook says Lassay

Saturday August 2nd 1986

Overcast but warmish

So far from Grandma's birthday money I have bought:-

Magazine/Book in French on WW2 secret services	25 Francs
1/72 scale Airfix astronauts	25 Francs
3 x C60 cassettes	7 Francs
FW 190 model kit (1/72 scale)	11½Francs
ESCI Afrika Korps (1/72 scale)	15 Francs
ESCI German infantry (1/72 scale)	12 ½Francs
Tight Fit cassette, inc The Lion Sleeps Tonight	11 Francs

plus others such as postcards, stamps, ice cream and pancakes.

I am owed 8.3 Francs by Beth. Will have in English as 80p

I am owed £6.50 by Mum, when back in England

I am owed 50p pocket money from Mum

I am owed £5 August pocket money from Dad

In addition to all that, I will get money from Grandma for doing well at my 'O' levels - £10 for an A, £5 for a B, and £1 for a C. I hope I do well - I don't really care about the money. It would be useful but I doubt I'd be allowed to spent much/most of it.

Also I will get 2 weeks wages for working at Thomas Cook from a week Monday. I hope this is enjoyable. It has a better chance of being so if I don't have to wear my ruddy suit. I hope it's better than working in Barclays Bank anyhow, like I did on work experience. The work was monotonous and I did most of it standing up. One got a lot of time for thinking. There, signing cheques I had checked for genuity [sic] I evolved my signature.

I hope to build all my 1/72 scale Germans into a cohesive force. The Afrika Korps - both new ASCI and old Airfix - will be converted and everything painted. Dad'll give me an area of the loft to set the whole lot up in one Special Force Siegreich (Victory). It will cost money for the paint and if possible other models and men, but hopefully I will have that money and be able to spend it.

Up around a quarter to 9. Shower. Went for a run and examination of the park attached to the stadium of which the campsite is a part. Rather good.

Left campsite. Stopped at supermarket where Mum and Dad did some shopping whilst Beth and I stayed in the camper. She read and I operated on all my ESCI soldiers, smoothing with my black-handled modelling knife their bases so that they all can stand up easily, straight, and fairly securely now. When I get home I will separate mortars from the men loading them, and stick their loaders onto a piece of card. I shall do the same with the large machine-gun gunners.

We drove to Bayeux, and spent 1 and three quarter hours in the tapestry museums. Reading a long and detailed history of what the tapestry shows - this was written in both French and English for, after all, with the large English connection the place is bound to get many British visitors, and does. A quarter hour documentary film on the tapestry - 1 in English, 1 in French. Finally seeing the tapestry itself in a darkened corridor-like room.

Dinner of French bread etc and an orange.

In the afternoon, Beth stayed in the camper. Mum and Dad went to the cathedral, but it happened to be shut for a wedding. I went to the Battle of Normandy museum - 5 to 10 minutes walk away. 3 tanks outside it on the grass - a German 'Hetzer', a British 'Churchill' and a US 'Sherman'. Cost 7 Francs to go in the museum - Mum had given me the money. Quarter hour film about the Battle of Normandy - 1 in English and later 1 in French. Many British people here. Very interesting with newspaper pages (many of which I read a lot from), uniforms on dummies, & arms - the German include a hand-held rocket-launcher like a bazooka, Schmeisser machine-pistols, potato-masher hand grenades, a large MG, a flamethrower, and a large 88mm gun. There were also some US vehicles, and a lifesize diorama of US soldiers. There was a 1/72 scale diorama on Falaise Pocket - not as interesting as it could have been. Interesting information on tanks, including German ones such as the Tiger, JagdPanther etc. There were posters of silhouettes.

There was nothing in the shop of affordable interest. Walked back to van. Arrived just in time. They were about to leave to look for me, but t managed to stop them. I had been gone for 3 HOURS!

We got lost looking for a campsite in Bayeux but eventually found it. Helped make tea of cheese pancakes, scalloped potatoes (both unfortunately got rather burned in the dry-fry), sweetcorn, plus a caramel custard. Listened to Nik Kershaw's 'The Riddle' whilst Mum and Dad did the washing up etc. Played 12 games of Speed - I lost disastrously to Mum, the winner on 43, and the others on 80.

Bed lateish.

Sunday August 3rd 1986

Overcast at first, poured with rain all morning, overcast and spitting the rest of the day.

Tomorrow we sail back to ENGLAND.

Up after half 8. Shower in smelly shower - not all that warm. Incident of me going to toilet in so-called women's WC in the row of cubicles. The men had only one normal loo and 2 hole-in-the-ground French ones. Arrived after breakfast and found the men's occupied. Waited a couple of minutes watching a French woman and her daughter play volleyball. Gave up waiting and went to a woman's WC - after all they're no different and for some reason they have a lot more of them. When I came out there were 3 women queuing and Mum who was very angry. TOTALLY UNJUST REALLY!

Left and drove in the pouring rain to Omaha Beach, a US landing beach on the 6th June 1944 Normandy landings. Thence on to Point du Hoc, a German fortified strongpoint near Omaha Beach, attacked by US troops scaling the cliffs after a naval bombardment. Got out here and wandered around, getting absolutely soaked. Rather interesting though. Took a couple of photos of the area. Then after getting changed we drove East to Arromanches - the site of the June 1944 Mulberry Harbour (artificial, towed across from Britain and set up off Arromanches to unload supplies for Allied troops before an operational port was captured).

Drove to a car park and had dinner of French bread etc and an orange. Dad and I went to the Arromanches museum - rather interesting. There were models of the harbour and a short documentary diorama with lights to show landings etc, plus a diorama of the landings somewhere which was very interesting to me, for it was in 25mm and also 1/72 scale and several groups of

Germans involved. There were weapons including a US mark 1 carbine, uniforms, and information.

Bought nothing from the not too-well-stocked and over-priced shop. Then we watched a documentary film in English about Mulberry Harbour. We left the museum after the film. Visited a couple of souvenir shops. In the second I bought for a total of 27 Francs (the last of my French money, and thus the last from Grandma) 2 books in French about German tanks and German motorised armour - half-tracks, assault guns etc.

We left and drove to Caen. Had a bit of food outside the chateau after an unsuccessful search for toilets. I finished 'Passenger to Frankfurt' - funny book, nothing like any of her others.

We drove to Ouistreham. We parked for the night in the queue of home-going British and a couple of adventurous French on the dockside. Long search for toilets. Tea of French smash, baked beans, French fish fingers, plus fruit cocktail.

Mum and Dad and me had conversation with others including a man in a large camper from Rutland. Firework display. Bed late.

Monday August 4th 1986

OK crossing, overcast, rain in the evening

72nd anniversary of the start of World War One including Britain.

Up about half past 6. Dressed and had a makeshift breakfast of French bread and apple juice. We didn't actually board the ferry (the Duc de Normandie, of Brittany Ferries, which I had seen at Portsmouth as we were leaving for France in July) till much later.

After search of ferry we set up around a table. For the first half an hour or more I read my books in French on WW2 German tanks. We had a game of speed, consisting of 12 rounds. As usual I was the loser, though by only 20 this time, and not 210 like the time before last! Mum won, I think.

I left the family and went and sat in the pullman lounge reading my book on German tanks.

Dinner of French bread, 2 plums, an orange and apple juice. After dinner I read again in a different section of the pullman lounge.

The Townsend Thoreson ferry 'Viking Venturer' preceded us into Portsmouth. I studied naval ships as we came in. To starboard were: F60 (Jupiter), P265 (Dumbarton Castle), F12 (Achilles), and Nottingham. Then 3 to port, 2 ahead, 2 further ahead. To starboard - F16 (Diomede), one I couldn't make out, and M109. There were many to starboard in the main section: F109 (Leander), F18 (Galatea), F70 (Apollo), D20 (Fife), F92 (Boxer), L11 (Intrepid). D12 (Kent) was to port.

We had a long wait before leaving the ferry and then we were searched by Customs. We left Portsmouth and drove towards

London. We paid a call on Grandma and found 3 ladies who had been playing bridge with her were just leaving. Another old lady who Grandma had known in Spain called Olive was staying with her. We had tea at Grandma's of bread with meat, Marmite, cheese and salad. Then hot cross buns then lovely cake, and I mean lovely for Grandma always makes lovely cakes. Then fruit from a can but in real juice and a cup of coffee.

Grandma gave me a wooden lion as a present - it being what she was presented with by her school governors, presumably on her retirement to go to Spain. Grandma is always giving away her ornaments and books for she has so many of them. In this way we have acquired several pieces of Lladro, some antique jugs, and in the realm of books Churchill's history of WW1 'The World Crisis' (dealing mainly with the navy for he was First Lord of the Admiralty), and around 20 Readers Digest books, mainly history such as 'Bohemia'.

Left Grandma's around 7pm. Down the road Aunty Mickie, Geraint and Howard saw us off half an hour later. Thanked them for my birthday present.

Drove home arriving around half past 10, after listening to Meatloaf and Nik Kershaw's 'The Riddle' on my personal stereo. Unloaded camper of essentials only as it was raining. Tandy greeted us. In the post waiting for us, I got a birthday card from Canada and from the Mullers in Gloucs who sent me £5.

Started sorting out soldiers. Bed tomorrow.

From Dad's Logbook

TOTAL MILEAGE	2342
Petrol	103 ¼ gallons
Cost of Petrol	£197.60
Number of Overnights	23
Cost of Overnights	£74.70
Entertainment	£27.25
Food	£107.40
Presents/Wine etc	£35.85
Miscellaneous	£15.40
Meals Out	£17.80
Necessities	£8.00
TOTAL	£484

THROUGH FRANCE TO ANDORRA

Brian G. Davies

I had long wished to re-visit Andorra. Over thirty years ago I had, with my parents, passed through on our way to the Costa Brava and had retained memories of clear skies, high mountains and - the shops. So, when examining all practical possibilities for our holiday last summer, Andorra came into the reckoning. I dug out the old 8mm movie I had taken on that earlier occasion and - presto; it was decided for me. My thirteen year old daughter insisted so go we did to Andorra, wife, teenage son and self also.

It was to be a strenuous though rewarding undertaking. I was fortunate enough to obtain three weeks leave from mid-July, and we needed every day of it. Weeks of route planning, obtaining the correct documents and preparing our six-berth Advantura motorhome culminated in our departure from Portsmouth on the early-morning Townsend Thoresen ferry bound for Le Havre. Many of us with motorhome or caravan had passed a satisfactory - and free - night on the Arrivals car park there, to be awakened in good time by the attendant, for the making of breakfast and other preparations before driving aboard about 8 a.m.

Six hours later, after a smooth and comfortable crossing, we had disembarked and were driving on the right (i.e. wrong to us) side of the road. This soon came naturally but my first error was in judging distances shown on the Michelin 1cm:2km map. Twice we turned off too early, before at last we crossed the impressive Tancerville bridge across the Seine estuary and headed for Blangy-le-Chateau, northeast of Lisieux. Here, another set-back; it was Bastille weekend and we had not booked ahead. However, we were well accommodated at the second site we tried, just south of the village which we later explored. The standard and style of architecture, and the general air of cleanliness was most impressive. Even the small pool/fountain on the central roundabout contained more than a dozen assorted fish - and no rubbish.

From here, things started to improve. Food was cheap and easily obtainable from sources ranging from village shops to giant hypermarkets. Throughout our journey, petrol was bought almost without exception on our Carte Bleu (VISA) so avoiding the need for extra cash or travellers' cheques. The only exception was, however, a hypermarket (Carrefour) outside Poitiers so, always check just in case. Our first visit of interest was the small hill-top village of Troo, famous for its troglodyte dwellings. The caves provided cool shelter from the afternoon heat and proved most interesting and the view from the escarpment across the plain dramatic. Soon we too were to be down there on the ribbon road en route for Vendome. Here, the municipal site on the banks of the Loire is an excellent stop-over, with simple hot FREE water, clean toilet areas, and a small shop. Being within easy walking distances of the town - with its church, castle and well-stocked shopping areas - and also adjacent to the local sports centre containing tennis courts and superb open-air swimming pool, we stayed here two nights. That evening being 14th July a firework extravaganza was held in the adjoining park to celebrate Bastille Day; it was an occasion not to be missed.

Vendome is within easy reached of the Loire valley with its many chateaux, any of which can provide a value-for-money visit into the past with their impressive buildings and magnificent furnishings. We chose Chenonceaux which, although actually on the river Cher, is regarded as one of the most important of the Loire valley castles. Here, parking is free and the building - once the home of Catherine de Medici and of Diana du Poitiers - offered much of interest to see

141

and learn about. We departed late that afternoon and, to make up the miles, had three hours hard driving before arriving for the night at the small town of Bellac, a little to the northwest of Limoges on the N 147. Here too the municipal site is well recommended, though our gremline struck again when (for the first time ever) we connected our camper to the site electricity. Suddenly, everyone in our particular section lost power, with fridges, televisions and lights all halting abruptly. Eventually power was restored but, despite an exhaustive investigation clearing us of blame, we were banned from further use, a set-back of no real hardship.

Whilst the war in France has been over for more than forty years it is not permitted to die in their memory. The small walled village of Oradour-sur-Glane, a little to the north-west of Limoges, is testimony to this. Known as the Martyr Village, it was the site on 10 June 1944 of one of the bloodiest atrocities by the SS during the whole of the German occupation. The village was systematically set alight and every inhabitant either shot or burned to death; over three hundred women and children died in the church alone. The scenes of desolation remain just as they were those forty-plus years ago, and will stay in our memories for a long time.

Limoges at siesta time was too hot for comfort so, after a quick visit to the bank for some much-needed money, we gave a miss to the famous enamel works and pressed on to Perigeux. Most of Holland appeared to be occupying the first site we tried so we moved on to Barnaby Plage, beautifully situated across the river Isle, with its two sections by a gondola-like ferryboat. It was with no little surprise that I came across the extensive - and popular - cafe/restaurant and the small crazy-golf area behind, and realised that I had previously visited that site some thirty-five years ago on that earlier trip to Andorra. Little had changed; even the patron had lived there in those days.

The road from Perigeux to Sarlat passes through limestone country with high cliffs, impressive gorges and many places of interest. Especially so are the Grotto du Grand Roc, a fantastic collection of stalactites/mites crammed into a cave over 50 metres up a cliff, and the Cro-Magnon remains at Les Eyzies. On to Cahors with its shady boulevardes and magnificent river, and down the N. 20 towards Montauban. Just north of here, at Albias, is an excellent private site with an immaculate swimming pool = providing the perfect end to a hot and tiring day. Next morning we decided to avoid the dense traffic of Toulouse and struck due east instead to Albi, a city situated on a huge sandstone outcrop. Albi appears to glow pink in the sunlight, its impressively-solid cathedral standing proudly in the centre, whilst across the river the old Gothic bridge brings us straight into the ancient quarter of the city.

Heading south down the N. 12, we branched off after Castres onto the D. 118 and into the lavender-growing areas surrounding Carcassonne. The site 'Les Lavandieres' outside the city a far better bet than the overcrowded stop-over at Le Stade nearer the centre. Next day an early start helped us to arrive ahead of the many tourists who would visit and view the impregnable walls, towers and castle of the old 'Cite' of Carcassonne, on the hill above the modern sprawl. Its narrow streets house souvenir shops and cafes by the score. No matter that much of the defences had been rebuilt in modern times (1844), the impression of mediaeval life is strong and it was reluctantly agreed that we departed to press ahead with the tortuous trail through Quillan and up over the Plateau de Sault to Ax les Thermes - the gateway to Andorra. Here there are several good sites but we settled for the municipal annexe at Orlu; if you prefer the peace of mountains and running water to the bustle of more populated areas this site in a quiet and pleasant valley is the one for you.

Despite leaving quite early for the climb into Andorra we still were caught up in the long queue winding its way slowly up the N. 20 towards the border. The views are however spectacular, and the 1 and a half hour climb seemed to pass quickly. Pas de le Casa was crowded with parked vehicles, and people taking advantage of its duty-free prices. We left them at it and headed for the Port d'Envalira, to enjoy a leisurely lunch with the Pyrenean peaks bathed in sunshine about us. We were there - in Andorra.

From here to Les Escaldes and the capital of Andorra la Vella it is downhill all the way. The country is a curious mixture of French and Spanish in all things - language, currencies, postal services and the people themselves. The north is predominantly French, the south Spanish and the centre a cosmopolitan mishmash of garages, construction, supermarkets and souvenir shops, all with their attendant people and vehicles. The noise and dust is incessant and we were glad to settle in on a site at Santa Coloma, where a nearby hotel allowed us to use their pool. However, next day we headed for the welcome peace of the small towns and settlements along the roads to the ski slopes. A very pleasant site at Pal caught our eye, complete with pool and bar, and excellent toilet facilities, all of which came in useful that evening.

Ten days had now passed and it was time to think about the return journey. Next morning was our son's sixteenth birthday so we celebrated with lunch at the Marco Polo restaurant in La Massana before pushing northwards once more towards the French border. On the way we visited the Sanctuary at Meritxell; destroyed by fire in 1976 it has been marvellously rebuilt on a grandiose scale, using glass and marble most effectively. It is only just off the main road, so don't miss it. Then up and on to Pas de la Case, arriving as the shops began to shut. Wild camping is permissible on the car park next to the border post, although toilet facilities are lacking everywhere except in the bars and hotels. However, no-one was churlish enough to refuse their use so a quiet and comfortable night was passed by all. Next day allowed us the opportunity for both shopping and sightseeing. Most of the town seems of haphazard construction, much still unfinished, and it presents an untidy and dirty appearance, but whisky at £2 a bottle (just one of the bargains) tends to offset such inconveniences. Then, crossing the last few metres to the border, we re-entered France and began the descent to Ax-les-Thermes, a spa town of no little interest and antiquity.

The drive along the Pyreneean foothills took us through Foix, with its 11th century castle perched on a rocky spur in the town's centre, to St. Girons and St. Gaudene, the latter a very clean and picturesque market town in the Garonne valley, with excellent shopping facilities and a superb view of the Pyrenees. Nearby is St. Bertrand de Comminges where we visited the old Roman church, the remains of the Roman settlement there, and then walked up to the cathedral perched on top of the rocky outcrop. Its richly-decorated interior is reputedly one of the most beautiful in Europe, with its wealth of carving and colour. After lunch we passed through the attractive spa town of Luchon (twinned with Harrogate) and onto the first of a series of cols to be traversed - the Col du Pyrenees, an exciting and rewarding run with its occasional surprises. The highest of these is the Col fu Tourmalet at over 2000 metres, whilst to traverse the Cirque de Litor on the Col d'Aubisque requires a cool head. On two occasions the road suddenly turns and dives into a rocky tunnel, hardly wide enough to accommodate a vehicle of our size. And with a motorhome the size of our Advantura there is no turning and retracing our steps.

Between these two passes we diverted to Lourdes, a city of two faces, secular and religious. The former is commercialism at its strongest, providing souvenirs of all types to the many thousands of tourists and pilgrims who visit each week. Crossing the bridge one enters the religious city, with its magnificent three-storeyed church

145

and the sacred grotto of St. Bernadette fame. Everywhere one sees the faithful, the crippled, the clergy and sightseers by the busfull. The overall impression is one of quiet intensity; a visit to Lourdes is like no other.

A few kilometres to the west lies the Betharram Grottos, cut out below ground in times past by the river Gerva. The visit consists of a cable-car ride up to the entrance, then a long guided walk through the grotto and its myriad calcinated deposits of all shapes and sizes. The commentary is pre-recorded and an English version is available if asked for. Then comes a long and winding descent through rock crevices, into a huge punt across an underground lake, and then - the final thrill - almost 2/3 of a mile in a ghost-train lookalike speeding through the semi-darkness over what was once the river bed. A truly fantastic - though quite expensive at £2.50 a head - visit to the underworld.

This part of France has its fair share of devotees to the Tour de France syndrome - groups of cyclists straining uphill, accompanied by their entourages. Other traffic comes to a standstill as they pass and village pavements are lined with cheering onlookers encouraging them on. On we went also, sadly having had to miss out on a trip to the impressively spectacular Cirque de Gavarnie on the Spanish border to the south of Lourdes. That night we stayed at Monplaisir, a quiet level site surrounded on three sides by high rocky peaks giving it an air of grandeur. Here, the cost of hot water is extra, but paid for at the time of booking. Beware; three of us had showers that evening, the next morning my wife could only get a cold shower, as the heating system was under repair.

Next day we entered Pau, a city where we found parking almost impossible but which boasts the mediaeval castle which was the birthplace of Henri IV. Shopping completed, including the purchase of red wine from the barrel (supply your own bottle) we carried on the Orthez, once the capital of the ancient province of Bearn, and now a pleasant market town. Then on through Dax to the Landes area and its Atlantic beaches and breezes. It was here that we forgot banks did not repoen until Tuesdays and nearly ran out of cash altogether. This situation was aggravated by the discovery that 'Bessie' had suffered a puncture and was listing quite badly. She remained like this throughout the night until at last a mechanic arrived from a Biarritz garage to set her right again. Thanks goodness for Europe Assistance... and for the warden of the 'Pomme de Pins'site at Seignosse, who kindly allowed us the use of his telephone.

The beaches along the coast seem endless, a long and glorious line of sand, sea, sun and sunseeking bodies, many topless and some - on selected beaches - nude. The pine forests lend an air of mystery and a pleasant fragrance to the day's travels, with here and there roadside glades set aside for picnicking, many equipped with purpose-built tables and benches. Just south of the Bay of Arcachon is found the Dune du Pilat, Europe's highest sand dune at over 117 metres. A long flight of wooden steps has been provided to assist the ascent, from the top of which one can gaze across the forest tops or out to sea, the Bay spread before you like a map. Arcachon itself was very crowded, with ample evidence on sale of the local delicacy - oysters, grown in the famous oyster beds of the Bassin d'Arcachon. Sites in the area are plentiful; we tried one at Bilos, south of Sallee, and were very pleased with its agreeable layout and forest surroundings, as well as the standard of facilities - shop included - as well as price.

As usual, we tried to give cities such as Bordeaux a miss, but all roads lead there, and in any case we needed a bank - again. However, we did not attempt the sights of the city on this occasion and headed for the N.10 and Angouleme, a charming mediaeval town with a most ornate cathedral, and on to Poitiers, an ancient town with Roman origins. At Chatellerault we diverted northwest

147

along the D.749 to Richelieu, an extremely charming walled village from which the French cardinal took his name, it being his birthplace. The municipal site here, though small, is new and of an excellent standard - and at the lowest price to date.

Next day saw us back in the Loire valley, initially visiting the small but attractive town of Chinon; its ruined castle boasts connections with both Richard the Lionheart and Joan of Arc. Nearby lies Fontrevaud Abbey - original burial place of four royal personages including Richard the First - and then on to the chateaux towns of Saumur and Angers. We still had many miles to travel and pressed on through Laval, Mayenne and Domfront, eventually calling a night halt at the small but excellent municipal site within a sports complex at Conde sur Noireau, a short distance before Caen. Surrounding the complex is attractive parkland which offers the visitor a chance to unwind after the day's exertions. Thirty miles north is the famed town of Bayeux, with its well-known tapestry museum, cathedral and museums of the 1940 Normandy landings. West of here lies Omaha beach, scene of the American landing on June 6th, and further west still the Pointe du Hoc where marines scaling the cliffs had eventually overcome the German forces dug in their concrete bunkers and gun emplacements. Turning eastwards the D-Day scenes are brought to life at Arromanches, once the site of the Mulberry Harbour. The museum here gives good value for its tour which includes models, press cuttings, a diorama and a film.

The city of Caen is dominated by its 11th century castle, built by William the Conqueror, as was the nearby Abbey au Hommes. Not to be outdone his queen, Matilda, founded the Abbey au Dames. Elsewhere is found the Fine Arts museum and of course the University. Though nominally the port from which Brittany Ferries depart for Portsmouth, the actual departure point is at the river's mouth, Ouistreham. Once more, our crossing was to be the first next morning so, together with other cars, caravans and campers, we joined the queue and prepared to spend the night. This was the port's first season in use following its reconstruction and the ferry's first season of operation. Late that evening we were treated to a splendid display of pyrotechnics, filling the night sky with their noise and colour. A really grand way to end the day... and to close our own grand visit to the continent. Altogether, we covered 2350 miles in 24 days, a truly unforgettable journey during which the motorhome behaved impeccably, the children were genuinely stimulated by their experiences, and we as a family gained from the need for tolerance and understanding when thrown together for so long. France is so full of superb scenery, interesting places to visit and excellent camp sites that we are looking forward to a further trip next year - though of more modest aims, Brittany, we think.

France 1987

Unfortunately my diary recording the first part of this holiday is lost. I have the diary from the last few days, and the logbook Dad always kept of our motorhome holidays, plus a selection of Dad's photographs, which he scanned in and sorted, and an album of my photographs. Dad's photographs are labelled, and mine were displayed in my album, so hopefully they have all been identified correctly, and placed in the right location in the narrative. I do remember taking photographs which have not, apparently, survived such as at Oradour-sur-Glane of the old cars on the street.

Some of what I remember most about this holiday is in the missing diary. This includes

1) We travelled to Calais by hovercraft, for the first and only time in me and my sister's experience (Mum and Dad may have done it before in the holiday they took without us in Easter 1979). I remember the hovercraft as fast but extremely loud.

2) Fouras, a coastal town, with a small fort, and a campsite in amongst the trees. I remember in the evening we walked the streets and I had the overwhelming feeling that everything was false, or fake in the world, except for the people living their lives in the houses we passed, some of which we could see into the basement floor of.

3) Sand dunes and sea, I don't recall where, though possibly Royan. I remember making my way through gorse in and out, whilst the others probably went to swim, then went back to the camper, but it was being successively blocked in by newly-arriving French vehicles, and I had to stand outside it and protect our way of egress, for what seemed like ages before the others returned.

I've pieced everything together as best I could. I was newly 17, and my sister was 14 and three quarters. We generally got on pretty well, lent each other music cassettes for our personal stereos, and chatted, or played cards at other times.

From Dad's logbook, the summary of the holiday is as follows:-

Overview of Campsites

August 1987	**Campsite**
8	Ferry port (Dover)
9	Deville, Rouen
10	La Fleche
11	Esnandes
12	Fouras
13	Tonnay-Charente
14	Tonnay-Charente
15	Moricq (nr Angles)
16	St Gervais (nr Beauvoir)
17	Madeline L'Etang
18	St Pierre, Dinan
19	Port Mer, St Malo
20	Sénéquet, Gouville
21	Ferry terminal, Cherbourg

Sunday 9th August 1987

05:40	Embark hovercraft
06:25	Depart Dover
	add 1 hour for continental time)
07:45	Arrive Calais
08:05	Depart
08:30	Cap Blanc Nez (visit Bunkers)
	Breakfast
10:00	Depart
	Visit Audinghen Museum
	Batterie Todt – 50 Francs
12:00	Depart
1.00pm	Arrive CU Montreuil-sur-Mer
	Lunch
2.05	Depart
2:45	Abbeyville
3.45	Petrol 194 Francs, Wine 11 Francs
3:55	Depart
4.45	Arrive Rouen
	Park and visit city centre
6:10	Depart
6:30	Arrive site (Déville – Municipal)
	Fee 51 Francs

150 miles

Cap Blanc Nez, Normandy – my sister and I bottom left, Mum
behind the tank

Mum by a German tank, Batterie Todt museum

Beth in ruined wall of German bunker, Pas de Calais, August 1987

Ruined German bunker,

Area of ruined German bunkers

The camper, Mum and Dad before the Pierre Corneille Bridge, Rouen

Monday 10th August 1987

11:00	Depart site
	Shopping
	via Elbeuf, le Neubourg
	Beaumont le Roger
	La Ferriere and Rugles
1:30	to l'Aigle
	Lunch (outside church)
2:30	Depart
3:30	Le Pin-la-Garenne - Toilets
	via Le Mans
5:30	Petrol 200 Francs @ 5.02 (39.6 litres)
5:40	La Fleche
	Visit Tourist Information Office
	Camping de la "Route d'Or"
	Fee 41.85 Francs

157 miles

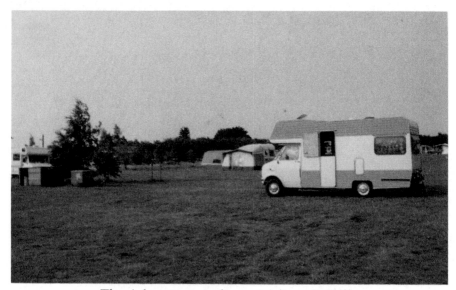

The Advantura on the campsite at Déville

Dad at La Fleche, midway between Le Mans and Angers

Tuesday 11th August 1987

10:55	Depart site
11:55	Angers
12:20	Stop for toilets (outside Wine Museum)
12:45	Start
	via Chalet and Montague
1:50	to Les Alouettes
	Lunch
3:45	Depart
	via Chantonnay
5:30	to Esnandes (Municipal)
	Fee 40 Francs

146 miles

Weather – warm, sunny/cloudy

Walk to sea in evening!

Cross and windmill at Les Herbiers, in the Vendée

From Wikipedia:-

Mont des Alouettes is a hill near Les Herbiers in Vendée, France. In the 16th century, no less than seven windmills were built on this hill. Today there are three left, one of which is still running. During the war in the Vendée the movement of the opposing troops were measured from the wind mills. Mont des Alouettes was the finish of the first stage of the 2011 Tour de France.

Les Herbiers, Vendee

I remember going to the museum about the Vendée, and reading about their history, especially in the French Revolutionary period where they stood out as one of the Royalist strongholds, until many of them were massacred by Revolutionary France. I bought the postcard below, from that museum, impressed with both the life of Jacques Cathelineau, leader in the war against the French Revolutionary forces, and his clothes!

The painting of Jacques Cathelineau by Anne-Louis Girodet de Roussy-Trioson, is in Versailles.

Water tower at Esnandes, and below our camper leaving the town

Wednesday 12th August 1987

9:20	Depart
10:00	Arrive Parking La Rochelle
	Elevenses on pavement by harbour
	Lunch
3:45	Depart
4:00	Arrive Leclerc Supermarket
5:45	Depart
6:15	Arrive site at Fouras
	Fee 44.60 Francs

31 miles

Our camper on the site at Esnandes

Candles in a church, La Rochelle

The port entrance at La Rochelle

Mum posing in La Rochelle

Harbour exit towers, La Rochelle

View from a harbour tower, La Rochelle

Boats in the harbour at La Rochelle

Dad's photograph of the castle/fort at Fouras

Postcard of Camping du Cadoret, Fouras, where we stayed

My photograph of the fort at Fouras

Thursday 13ᵗʰ August 1987

10:45	Depart site
10:55	Arrive Parking
	Watch oyster beds and shells
11:35	Depart
11:45	Arrive Grande Plage
	Visit Fort Enet
	Lunch
	Beach – Dad, Jon and Beth
	Dad + Beth swim – cafe
16:30	Depart
18:00	Arrive Tonnay-Charente
	Fee 30.50 Francs

16 miles

Me, Beth and Mum watching the oyster fishing, photo by Dad

Boats oyster fishing

The campsite at Tonnay-Charente

Beth in the camper, probably making dinner

Friday 14ᵗʰ August 1987

11:00	Depart site
11:30	Rochefort
	Shopping
12:40	Depart
	Petrol – 29.3 litres
	via Pont de la Seudre (16.40 Francs)
1:40	to Ronce les Bains
	Lunch in forest
3:25	Depart
3:45	Pharos de Coubre
	Walk on/around beach
5:15	Depart
5:55	via Royan
6:20	Call at Pineau-Cognac Distillery
6:55	Depart
7:30	Arrive suspension bridge
7:50	Depart
8:05	Arrive camp site
	(@ Tonnay-Charente)
	Fee 30.50 Francs

86 miles

Saturday 15th August 1987

10:40	Depart site
11:15	Chatelaillon plage
	Swim in sea. Walk on beach
1:55	Depart
2:25	Angoulins
	Lunch
3:40	Depart
4:15	La Rochelle – Petrol

40 litres as 5.1 Francs per litre, 204 Francs

Petrol station would not accept credit card.
Had to get cash from Supermarket

via L'Aiguillon-sur-mer to

| 5:30 | Moricq (near Angles) |
| | Fee 36.4 Francs |

88 miles

Chatelaillon , with Dad looking down

Chatelaillon, with Mum, Dad and Beth on the beach

Sunday 16th August 1987

10:50	Depart
	Shopping
	visit Brocante in Angles
11:50	Depart
	via Les Sables d'Olonne
1:00	Arrive Sauveterre
	Lunch and swim
3:00	Depart
4:35	Entrance to Isle de Noirmoutier
5:00	Ville de Noirmoutier
	on to l'Herbaudiere (port)
6:40	Depart
6:55	Barbatre
	Shopping
7:10	Depart
	Cross by Le Goise and watch water rise
7:50	Depart
8:05	Arrive site at Saint Gervais
	Fee 32 Francs

101 miles

Big electrical storm overnight

The Brocante at Angles – sadly it is not there anymore, though the building remains and is in use as a ping-pong hall

A Citroen estate at the Brocante at Angles – this type of car was the one I wrote into the story I wrote for a while

Crossing by Le Goise, the causeway from Noirmoutier

The Passage du Gois is a causeway between Beauvoir-sur-Mer and the island of Noirmoutier, in Vendée on the Atlantic coast of France. The causeway is 4.125 kilometres (2.6 mi) long and is flooded twice a day by the high tide. A road runs along the causeway.

My Memory

We went on the causeway to the Isle de Noirmoutier, and on the way back there was some delay, with us having to park up on it, and wait. I was dying for the loo, but discovered that drinking more weirdly took my thoughts away from this, and had a cup of instant coffee whilst we waited.

Looking sideways off the causeway

Mum on the causeway, in the door of the camper with a coffee

Still on the Causeway

On the causeway from the Ile de Noirmoutier

Monday 17th August 1987

11:30	Depart
12:30	Arrive Pornic
	Shopping
	Lunch
15:45	Depart
16:00	Le Porteau
16:10	Depart
16:45	Pont St Nazaire – Toll 30 Francs
17:00	St. Nazaire
17:10	Stop at harbour
	Coffee and walk
18:00	Depart
18:25	Pornichet
	Petrol
	via La Baule
	and to le Pouliguen and Guerande
20:00	to site at L'Etang
	Fee 71.60 Francs

81 miles

Mum at Pornic

Saint Nazaire

Monday August 17ᵗʰ 1987

Sunnyish and quite hot but more wind

C(+)

Bed now because of flies and itchy.

Well it rained and thundered and lightning all night - a very odd experience, and now in the morning, I find strange puddles of water where objects press down upon the groundsheet and pressure it.

Now, going and seeing if I can have a shower - hopefully warm, not that it's cold, but because I dislike cold showers (cold after warm I usually do at the end at home to make drying myself easier).

As it's c11pm now and I'm on my sleeping bag in the camper with my personal stereo on listening to one of Beth's cassettes - compilation of recent pop from off the radio, excellent for ALL are good songs (including 'It's A Sin', 'You're The Voice', 'Hold Me Now'). Beth for some reason is at the other end of my bed so I am a bit squashed. Dad's looking at a book and map of Brittany and Mum at present is at the toilet block. Starship's excellent "Nothing's Gonna Stop Us Now" is playing on the personal stereo now.

After a thunder, lightning, rain of a night, up before Dad came at half 8 p.m. Shower. Breakfast of prunes and toast. Put tent away. Took photo for Beth of an interesting dog.

We drove off North to PORNIC where we parked and Mum and Dad went to a supermarket, I and Beth went around town. Posted postcards to Andrew, Grandma, and to Grandad. Bought L'Equipe, French sports newspaper. In football, Monaco are top of Division 1, after they beat Toulouse 5-1 yesterday with 2 goals by Hately and 1 by Waddle.

Then we drove on a little and all went a bit round town, but Beth insisted she and I return soon after so we did (I had Mum's spare key). Back, I wrote newly-purchased postcards to Mark, and later to Aunty Beryl and Uncle Dave, and to Giles. When all were back, we had dinner of bread (French-pain) etc and an orange. Then we left and drove on Northwards.

We stopped soon after nowhere in particular but near a popular beach we gazed down upon. We continued North and over the bridge at Saint Nazaire (bloody weird) into the city where we stopped by the sea. Coffee, then Mum and Dad walked. I listened to my personal stereo (Beth's Meatloaf cassette).

We drove North and got confusingly lost somewhere, in a city, and finally found a very expensive campsite (L'Etang) for £7 (!) but nice and pleasant. We were near 4 or 5 other lots of British people, and also a heavy Dutch presence. Here we made tea - quiche, beans, harricot vert, and tinned peaches. Beth and I did the dishes, while Mum and Dad walked.

The photo of an interesting dog (on a car roof!) I took for Beth

Mum reading on the Du Port au Bois de Porcé, Saint Nazaire

The campsite at L'Etang

Tuesday 18th August 1987

11:15	Depart site
11:45	Arrive Guerande
	Visit walled town – shopping
1:45	Depart
2:30	Camoel
	Lunch
3:30	Depart
4:30	Ploermel
5:30	Caulnes
5:50	Dinan
7:20	Depart
7:55	Arrive site at St. Pierre de Plerguen
	(near Dinan)
	Fee 19.10 Francs

118 miles

Tuesday August 18th 1987

Cold and dull at start, turning warmer and sunnyish

Bed c 11 perhaps

C(+)

\\\ RUDOLPH HESS DIES /// - Aged 93. Suicide likely.

It's late at night now, after half past 10pm anyway, and I'm on a stone table with my feet on a wooden bench at the campsite tonight. Thanks to a sudden reminder by Beth, a quick decision by me, and quick work by both of us, my tent was erected in semi-darkness and I will sleep there tonight. (I had a difficult night last night in the camper).

Today I found an English Sunday newspaper and saw Saturday's football results:-

Division 1

Arsenal 1 Liverpool 2

Everton beat someone I have forgotten 1-0

Division 2

Manchester City 2 Plymouth 0

Bradford City 2 Swindon Town 0

Division 4

Torquay 6 Wrexham 1 - Guess that means Torquay are top after 1 game, on goal difference

Orient 1 Cardiff 1

Wolves 2 Scarborough 2

Hartlepool drew 0-0 with someone

However, before I could find out any others and find the actual results page, the shop bloke came up, snatched the paper from me and delivered an ultimatum - 14 Francs he said. I made a "You must be joking!" noise and left the shop. I wasn't going to buy it so I suppose he was justified but no one would buy it at that price. If it was reasonably priced, 8 Francs or less, I would probably have bought it but as it was - NO WAY!

What about today? Weather-wise I liked it - cooler and duller at first and not as hot as before in the rest of the day. But it is not cold so I can sit here on the table at this time of night in shorts and a t-shirt.

TODAY

Up and showered and breakfast of cereal (French 'banana' cornflakes) and toast. We drove to GUERANDE from the campsite of L'Etang. This walled city was OK but mainly shops - church too, but it was only OK. Found GB newspaper but 'roughly' treated by shopowner over it. We left and walked outside walls (only forms the nucleus of the town, as in York, Chester etc).

Drove to Leclerc supermarket where I bought a notebook. Beth and I then in camper while Mum and Dad did the shopping.

The walls of Guerande, and below a ruined tower on them

Porte Saint-Michel, Guerande

Then, after a lot of the usual getting lost, had dinner in the woods on the road to Camoel. Drove North a long way to Dinan, during which I lay down at the back and listened to "Chance +" cassette on the camper's cassette player and slept a bit.

We walked round Dinan, I getting separated but finding them at the camper after I'd found a shop with old records (BUT £2 each at least - bloody pathetic!).

We got lost looking for campsite so drove in a little to here - St. Pierre Plesguen. Small, but adequate and peaceful, and cheap. Started reading "Anglo Saxon Attitudes" again for school, but not too thrilled. Tea of cabbage, sausage etc from tins, and potato waffle and apple pastry and custard from carton - lovely! Beth and I did dishes while Mum and Dad went for a walk. Listened to music and put up the tent. Brushed teeth and washed. Sat on stone table listening to personal stereo and wrote this.

Doing the dishes on a campsite, I don't look too thrilled!

Wednesday 19th August 1987

10:50	Depart
	Petrol in village
11:15	Chateauneuf
	Bank – change 200 Franc Travellers Cheque, and £50 cash into 476 Francs
11:25	Depart
11:55	St. Malo – port
	Park / Lunch
3:40	Depart
3:55	Arrive Lupin
	Swim etc on beach
5:45	Depart
6:!5	Le Grouin
6:45	Depart
6:50	Site at Port Mer
	Fee 43 Francs

34 miles

Wednesday August 19th 1987

Dull start getting hot and sunny by Midday

C+

BLOKE IN HUNGERFORD (Thames Valley) - Michael Ryan

MAD IT SEEMS SHOOTING PEOPLE

9 Killed, 14 injured, Centre cordoned off

(Final total of 16 including himself)

Torch batteries are still surviving, just, or I wouldn't be able to write this, and batteries for personal stereo still survive too, though for not much longer I believe. However, Mum and Dad bought us more on Tuesday (today as I write this introduction yesterday) so I'll be OK for the rest of the holiday and the ferry crossing (5 HOURS! EARLY MORNING! Won't like it one bit and we've forgotten travel sickness tablets. However, we shall see) if I am lucky and careful, I suppose.

I had a rather interesting discussion with Beth this evening about what is important in life. She said HAPPINESS and as for why - if you're not happy you think life's not worth living so happiness is necessary to make life worthwhile. Some people like being sad but I suppose it makes them happy being so. We discussed God - not the matter of His existence, but His vanity - always wanting to be praised and won't countenance any other being worshipped (even if they exist?). We thought of a funny scenario - Moses receiving the Ten Commandments: "You shall have no other God but me". "Why?" he asks. Very good question. We went no further.

TODAY

Didn't sleep too well for sleeping the wrong way [round] but somehow managed. Awoken by Dad. Breakfast on the stone table outside - rather posery I felt, but I would have done it for fun/laugh in their place. Beth and I did dishes.

A meal on the stone table outside

We drove North to Saint Malo after a visit to the garage and bank, in the spare bits of which time I wrote more of the fictional war story.

Arrived in Saint Malo and parked near several huge German motorhomes. Walked into and round the old walled city, having dinner at a restaurant there - gaulettes (similar to oat cakes), with fillings (mine was cheese, egg, and onions) and (for me) a little pot of ice cream and crepes (pancakes) with honey.

Walked out and across, back to a fort we didn't go round, and then back to the camper. All this in St. Malo took a few hours.

View at Saint Malo

Drove off along coast Eastwards to Lupin, where went to the beach.

While Mum sunbathed and Dad and Beth swam, I climbed rocks to sit in a little woods. Tried to read or write, but couldn't be bothered. Went back to camper and listened to Beth's "Star Trekkin' +" cassette, till all returned and we drove on, looking at campsites but stopping at viewing places and rocks to look at the view.

Then we drove downhill to a campsite, where we are now. Tea of bread etc and yoghurt. Beth, Mum, and I did dishes. Mum and Dad went out to the showers and Beth and I remained in and listened to music and talked. We all played scoring whist (bid etc) with 13-1 cards. I and Beth joint winners with 105 points (Dad 3rd, Mum last). Mum and Dad went out for a walk, and Beth and I played my variations of rummy. Parents returned, and we 2 washed at washrooms down the hill.

Bed and wrote this lot laying on bed, listening to Nik Kershaw.

195

Harbour at St. Malo (the Vauban Basin)

Saint Malo

Saint Malo - row of large motorhomes in the carpark

Gate - entrance to the old area of Saint Malo

Dilapidated tower in the walls of old Saint Malo

Corner of the wall walk of the old walls of Saint Malo

Beth and Mum in the sea at Lupin

Near Port Mer

Thursday 20th August 1987

10:35	Depart
11:35	Pontorson
12:00	Mont St. Michel
	Visit ville
	Buy card and adhesive
3:00	Depart
	Shop at supermarket
3:30	Depart
4:20	Granville
6:00	Gouville
	Site at Sénéquet
	Swim on beach (across road)
	Fee 32.90 Francs

89 miles

Thursday August 20th 1987

Sunny and hot, cooler night than before

More financial troubles in the City as borrowing higher than expected. More share price decreasings. Is this really worrying?

Next-to-last full day in France as we leave early Saturday.

Can't write much tonight because the torch won't last long enough, I suspect. Yes, I AM in the tent tonight, but in my pyjamas sat on a deck chair between the tent and the camper, and write this listening to Nik Kershaw on my personal stereo.

TODAY

Up and washed and toileted at the funny washroom/toilet area. Breakfast of cereal (some sultana bran with cornflakes) and toast.

We drove to the viewpoint again so the others could go to the toilet, which are English style there and clean. At the campsite all were French style - the hole in the ground - and the others said they were dirty, though I didn't notice.

We drove to Mont St Michel, I listening to Human Racing cassette a few times on the personal stereo. At Mont St Michel we parked in a large car park by the edge of a causeway and walked to and round the "town", not going in churches as you had to pay, nor museums. A church struck me with an atmosphere resultant of dimness, candles and strange choir music playing and I took a photo with Beth's camera.

I was anyway content to walk around the wall walks and sloping roads. I felt the place was OK though much too extremely touristised.

After dinner of bread etc in the car park we drove Northwards through Normandy towards Cherbourg, I listening to The Riddle and Human Racing cassettes, and Beth to the Bon Jovi one recorded off my album.

We went fast - 60mph, the fastest I've ever seen the camper at, at stages - behind other British vehicles, dangerous Swiss motorbikes, pesky French caravans, arrogant lorries, and later crawled behind big wagons, which made the journey less enjoyable. We were not too far from the peninsular when we decided to look for a campsite and found one.

Beth, Mum and Dad went off to the sea to swim, but I resisted the pressure and with a little help from Dad, at first, erected the tent. While they were gone, I made my bed, did the dishes (remnants of dinner), laid the table and sorted out my bag. I'll probably give my parents my 20 Franc note in exchange for £2, which would mean I'd have £11 on me, £2 owed by Mum (pocket money), £5 from Dad at start of September, and £5 from earnings then. I hope to buy U2's album 'The Joshua Tree' when we get back.

Tea of chips bought, petit pois and scrambled egg and tinned peaches and rice pudding. Did dishes. We played solo whist again and I came second (Beth won, a close-run thing, I could've come joint top again. Mum was last and Dad was 3rd).

Dad and Mum went for a walk around the campsite. Beth and I played various versions of rummy. We went off to the toilet block when parents returned. I had a quick shower. Came back and wrote this. Bed rather late

Queuing at Mont Saint Michel

Visiting Mont Saint Michel, Dad in the foreground

Postcard of Mont St. Michel, mentioned in the text

Swimming at Senequet

Friday 21st August 1987

10:40	Depart
12:00	Cherbourg supermarket
	Shopping (Continent)
	Lunch
5:00	Depart – east
5:50	Arrive Fermanville
	Small harbour (+ cat)
	Got very dark and stormy
6:50	Depart
7:10	Arrive Continental supermarket
Cherbourg	
	Arrive at port

Sleep overnight at Terminal carpark

Heavy thunderstorm at terminal

83 miles

Friday August 21st 1987

Last Full Day in France

Duller and cooler, rained with fog late afternoon, thunder and lightning and heavy rain in the evening, dry and OK by nightfall

C+

I sit in bed in the camper with my back up against the wall, at just before 11p.m. Mum and Beth are at the toilets and Dad talks to a man in the car in front of us. We are at Cherbourg Docks and 2nd in line for Weymouth line for early tomorrow morning. There is another line to our right and both consist mainly of cars with caravans. The car immediately to our right is a dark Saab.

TODAY

This morning, up by Dad and had a shower ere breakfast. Put tent down. We drove North towards Cherbourg, I listening to Nik Kershaw on the personal stereo. When we got there we drove around and found a Maxi Coop supermarket. Pretty useless but some reduced records (c £1 each - 2nd cheapest I've see here). I bought Queen's "The Hammer to Fall" (1984) with my last Francs, exclusive of my 20 Francs which I gave Mum for £2 later.

We drove to a big CONTINENT supermarket where I walked round and got bored and returned to the camper, the others taking ages to come back, because of buying wine etc. I searched medium wave bands for radio stations and found several English ones, including Radio 2 I think (useful for football results tomorrow - NB, Spurs beat Newcastle 3-1, and Man Utd and QPR drew on Wednesday, I heard on the radio yesterday).

We drove after dinner to a small fishing village where we had coffee. Mum and Dad went for a walk, and Beth and I played cards. An upset Siamese cat found us and Mum and Beth delivered it to a nearby house - owners gave us flowers.

We drove back to Cherbourg and CONTINENT for toilets, then drove to the port where we parked in the camping area. Beth and I played cards and talked - an enjoyable discussion on politics and nuclear weapons.

Tea of carrots and ratatouille, peaches and chocolate sauce. Dried dishes.

We moved up to the lines for the ferry tomorrow.

Saturday 22nd August

4:30am	Move through Control to Embarkation Point
5:00	Embark
5:45	Depart *French time
9:00	Arrive Weymouth
9:15	Disembark
	Through customs – no delay
9:30	Dorchester
	Petrol 31 litres
	via Cerne Abbas
10:10	Stop on A352
10:45	Depart
11:15	Stalbridge – visit estate
12:45	Woodhenge
2:10	Savernake Forest (Grand Avenue)
	Lunch near Hungerford
2:55	Depart (via Janet's etc) / Petrol
4:30	Oxford
6:00	Northampton
7:20	Arrive home (Peterborough)

223 miles

Saturday 22nd August 1987

Rain and thunder/lightning with sunny spells

C - illish feeling, perhaps a residue of the ferry

Up rather ruddy early (c 04:30) for time to move forward and soon board the ferry. Taking a plastic bag of assorted things I went up with the others and we sat in some not uncomfortable seats facing backwards starboardwise in a lounge/seating area. For most of the journey, sat there and listened to personal stereo (mainly Nik Kershaw) and read Victoria Holt's "The Curse of the Kings" - very good/interesting (perhaps more so for people and relation between those archaeological, ancient Egyptian history but. Got to "know" and "like" characters, especially Hadrian, Sabina and Theodosia, and Sir Ralph. The type of thing I like to be able to do in books).

On my occasional wanderings I did not feel too well because of the roll of the ship. I stood on the stern deck in the rain in my t-shirt looking out.

We arrived at Weymouth c9 a.m. English time, and drove through the town into Dorset where we visited Stalbridge (the village we used to live in) and saw Meadow Close and our house at the bottom.

We drove past Stonehenge and Salisbury Plain to Woodhenge, where we went around it, and I ran round in circles for a bit of exercise for once. We drove on and had dinner in Savernake Forest (where Michael Ryan shot his first victim) before going to Hungerford itself and calling on Aunty Janet and family who were, however, out. We drove North-Easterly home via Oundle and arrived in rain.

We unpacked and Janet phoned. We'd missed them by five minutes - her, Uncle Dick, and their daughter Noni. She told Mum all about the past year and their 3 children (aged 25, 20, and Noni at 15) and how she had been shot at by Ryan but missed.

I listened to new records - all good. Tea of chips and beefburger

Bath and read a bit of Herodotus. Bed after 11pm.

From Dad's Logbook

TOTAL MILEAGE	1609
Petrol	71 ½ gallons
Cost of Petrol	£152
Number of Overnights	11
Cost of Overnights	£48.56
Entertainment	£5.13
Food	£61.38
Presents/Wine etc	£30.63
Miscellaneous	£12.47
Drinks/Meals Out	£19.45
Tolls and Parking	£6.33
TOTAL	£335.95

Conversion rate at 9.75 Francs to £1

About the Author

Jon N. Davies was born in Leeds, first went to school in Dorset, and grew up in Peterborough. He gained a BA (Hons) in History from Royal Holloway. These days he lives in his ancestral homeland of South Wales, and writes local history, naval history, and family history.

When his father was dying in 2022, he promised he would produce a series of books to honour the family legacy, of which this volume is the fifth. He believes that the past should be remembered, and hopes that the future will remember the present in turn.

His other works include 'The Goughs of Ynyscedwyn', a compendium of articles that first appeared in Infinity Wanderers magazine, covering the Gough squires of that estate, and their Portrey predecessors, from the late 17th century up to 1835. He continues to work on the later period, with part 2 of his life of Richard Douglas Gough (1796 to 1886) appearing in issue 10 of Infinity Wanderers in Summer 2024.

Childhood Home is a One Place Study of 2 Juniper, the house the author grew up in, from its purchase as a new-build in 1976, to 1995 when his parents sold it. It consists, so far, of 3 volumes:- The First Ten Years, The Near Environs, and The Final Decade.

Touching Paradise is a book on the villa his paternal grandparents built in Spain, in the mountains behind Fuengirola, in the 1960s, and covers its development until they sold it in the late 1970s.

Thank You to my sister, Beth, for supporting these works.

Jon, and the family cat Tandy (1978-1994) in better times

Remembering Mum and Dad

Maureen Davies was born on 8th February 1941, and passed away on 29th April 2014, aged 73, at Knighton Community Hospital.

Brian Gwilym Davies was born on the 25th September 1933, and passed away on 19th January 2022, aged 88, in Morriston Hospital, Swansea.

Mum and Dad in front of the Advantura, at 2 Juniper, Peterborough

Maureen and Brian Davies are buried in the New Cemetery, Knighton, Powys.

Printed in Great Britain
by Amazon

41991041R00119